the doctrine of SALVATION

C. B. Hogue

CONVENTION PRESS
Nashville, Tennessee

5133-09

This book is the text for a course
in the subject area Baptist Doctrine
in the Church Study Course

Dewey Decimal Classification Number: 234
Subject: SALVATION

Printed in the United States of America

Editors: *Bill Latham and Nolan P. Howington*
Manuscript Assistant: *Anne M. Donahue*
Artist-Designer: *Clyde T. Denton, Jr.*

About the Author

C. B. Hogue is known and respected by Southern Baptists in all walks of life. Leaders and laypersons alike identify Dr. Hogue with evangelism because of his skill and dedicated leadership as director of the evangelism section for the Home Mission Board of the Southern Baptist Convention.

Dr. Hogue received the B.A. and D.D. degrees from Howard Payne College and the B.D. degree from Southwestern Baptist Theological Seminary. Before assuming his present responsibility, he served as a pastor in Texas and as a pastor and as state director of evangelism in Oklahoma.

Contents

Three Ways to Study This Book

LARGE GROUP STUDY

This book is the text for Baptist Doctrine Study 1979. Most of the studies will be conducted in groups of twenty-five or more. These large group sessions will be more effective if the leader will adapt the small group study guides for use by a larger group and use the teaching aids in *The Doctrine of Salvation Resource Kit* (item 5123-09 on the Undated Materials Order Form).

SMALL GROUP STUDY

Church Training groups or other small groups can study this book by using the directions for leading small group sessions. These guides are at the end of the text and give directions for five one-hour sessions.

INDIVIDUAL STUDY

You can study this book on your own as well as in a group. Carefully work through each chapter, completing each Personal Learning Activity as it appears in the text. You will be introduced to fresh ideas. Take time to consider and to evaluate each one.

Requirements for receiving credit in the Church Study Course for the study of this book are at the end of the text. *(See table of Contents.)*

Salvation

In the New Testament, salvation means deliverance from the power, guilt, and penalty of sin. Through the sacrificial death of Christ God rescues us from evil's dominion, reconciles us to himself, makes us whole persons, and sets our feet in the way of righteousness. Personal salvation is, however, contingent upon man's response in repentance and faith. It is God's gracious gift, but the gift must be freely received.

Salvation has three dimensions:

1. It is a past event and refers to what God has done for us in Christ.
2. It is a present reality which we experience and by which our lives are changed.
3. It is a future expectation, looking to ultimate redemption and our life with Christ in his glory.

Nolan P. Howington

Introduction

This book grows out of the need for a clear, definitive statement of what God is doing on behalf of the human race. The heart of religious experience is the fact of redemption: humanity's need for redemption, what God has done and is doing to provide that redemption, and the effect redemption should have on persons and on society. In today's world, the great variety of religious sects, doctrinal theories, and emotional expressions have obscured the simple, basic truths about redemption. This book is an effort to restate simply and systematically the doctrine of salvation.

The study begins at the point of man's desperate need for help that he cannot give himself. Chapter 1 is a study of what mankind is doing to himself (corruptive wrongdoing), why he is doing it (his inner inconsistency with the holiness of God), and where it is leading him (alienation from himself, from others, and from God, both now and eternally).

Chapter 2 shows that God's intent has always been the redemption of all his creation, but especially persons. Since evil has defeated man's ability to act responsibly, God does act responsibly out of love. He takes the initiative to do what has to be done to bring man back to the God in whose image man was created and in whom man is intended to find completeness.

Chapter 3 shows how God acted in Christ to do all that was necessary to provide salvation, and chapter 4 shows how the enabling action of the Holy Spirit is essential to the salvation experience. It is the Holy Spirit who makes us aware of our need, who enables us to believe, who breathes new life into us, and who sustains and assures us in the new life in Christ.

It is important to understand that persons do not bring salvation to pass because they take the initiative in seeking out and in finding God. Chapter 5 shows that salvation takes place because man responds to the initiative God took in the incarnation, the crucifixion, and the resurrection. That response is repentance and faith.

BLAIR SEITZ

The heart of religious experience is the fact of humanity's need for redemption and what God has done and is doing to provide redemption.

The changes produced by salvation are so numerous, so radical, and so far-reaching that no single word or phrase can describe them all fully. A number of words or phrases are used to list, to differentiate, and to define the many changes that are a part of the salvation experience. Chapter 6 is a study of some of these words and phrases that define the different aspects of the salvation experience.

The new life in Christ must express itself as surely as our physical bodies must breathe. To refuse or to stifle this expression is to smother the very life out of the believer's newfound joy. Chapter 7 deals with three settings in which the Christian life expresses itself: the church, the home, and the community.

Christianity is a way of life. But it is a way of life that moves toward a definite goal. That goal is a joyful consummation in which the believer will experience all that he has waited for in faith. The final chapter discusses what the life beyond this life holds in store and the meaning of the ultimate fulfillment that awaits the believer in the life beyond this life.

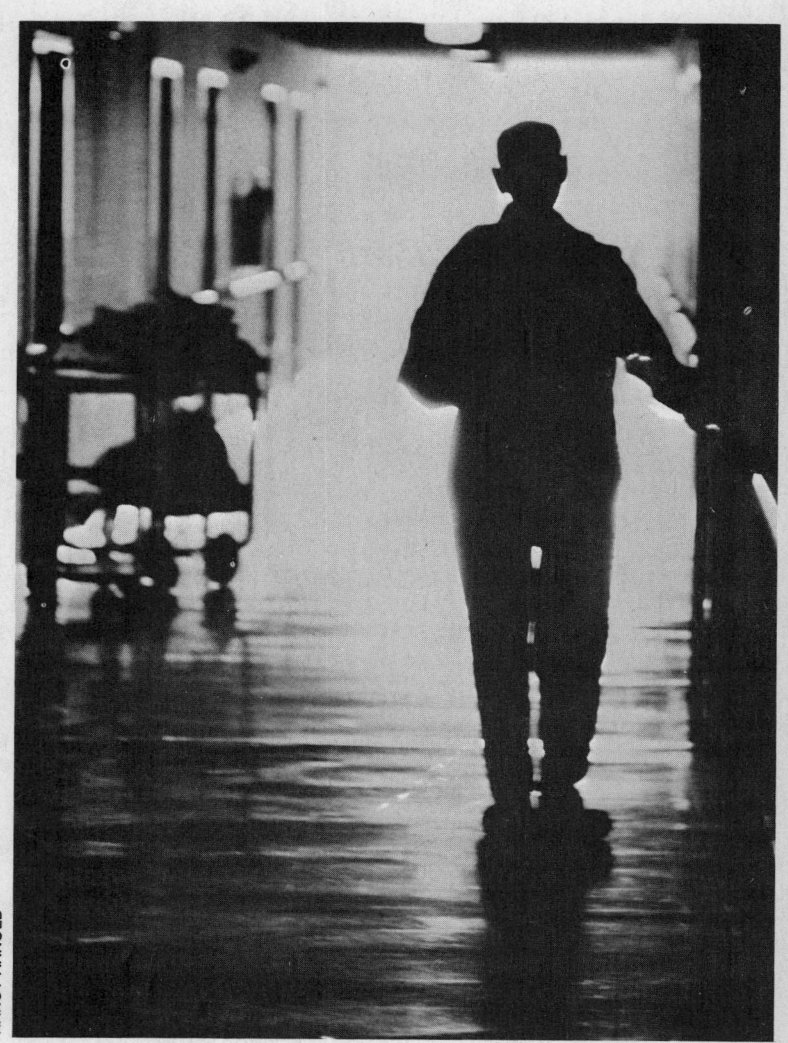

NANCY ARNOLD

The evidence of what persons are doing to themselves and to one another is evidence enough that something is gravely wrong with mankind.

Chapter 1

Salvation: Man's Paramount Need

There's good news, and there's bad news. The bad news is that man is a sinner. Man's inhumanity to man testifies to the fact. The repetition of human failure and hopelessness and despair is a result of man's being a sinner. The bad news is even worse because it is impossible for man to help himself in his plight. Man is a sinner, and he needs help. That's bad news. But there's good news, too. God has come to the rescue.

This chapter is about the bad news and why it is that way. Perhaps that is a depressing or an alarming way to begin a book, but this is where we are. Humanity is faced with a threefold problem: (1) what man is doing to himself, (2) why he does it, and (3) where it all is leading. This is a desperate situation, because it is one for which there is no human solution. It is a situation in which each person finds himself and from which each person needs to be rescued. This is why the purpose of this chapter is to show that persons are sinners in need of a Savior and that salvation is mankind's paramount need.

WHAT MAN IS DOING TO HIMSELF

As good a term as any to express the nature of what man is doing to himself is *corruptive wrongdoing*. Corruptive wrongdoing is described by the Christian community as sin. It is a fact of history that all religions have been concerned with the question of what we describe as sin—its origin and its abolition. In all periods of time, even the best of people admit to sinfulness when they are confronted by truth.

The Sins Men Do

Although we have only the word *sin,* the Scriptures use a variety of words to describe the different aspects of sin. In the Scriptures the writer would choose the word that best expressed the particular aspect of sin he wished to emphasize. The word used most often by both Old Testament writers and New Testament writers expressed the idea of transgressing or doing wrong. It is these sins—the sins of action—that are most apparent. It is also these sins that we think about first when we consider sin.

PERSONAL LEARNING ACTIVITY 1

Read Romans 1:18 to 3:20 and note the emphasis on doing wrong deeds. Divide a sheet of paper into three columns. In the first column, recall and list at least eight instances of wrongdoing that are recorded in the Scriptures. In the second column, list instances of wrongdoing that are reported on the front page of your newspaper. In the third column, list instances of wrongdoing in your own life that have occurred within the past week.

If there were no other evidence to offer, the evidence of what persons are doing to themselves and to one another is evidence enough that something is gravely wrong with mankind. All cannot be well when the fabric of life is permeated with corruptive wrongdoing. Both the Old Testament (Ps. 14:2-3; Eccl. 7:20; Isa. 53:4-6) and the New Testament (Rom. 3:10-23; Gal. 3:22; 1 John 1:8) make it quite plain that every person is a participant in humanity's practice of corruptive wrongdoing.

The Seriousness of the Sins Men Do

We have a tendency to reason away some of or most of the seriousness of what we are doing to ourselves and to one another. This is not impossible to do so long as we see the wrongs we do only as wrongs against ourselves or as wrongs against others. Then the wrongs can be regarded as partly deserved, or as something that can be straightened out later, or as something that is not as serious as it appears. The seriousness of the sins men do lies in the fact that far more is involved than this reasoning permits. We need to realize that every sin is a sin against God.

Beginning with Cain's inhumanity to Abel (Gen. 4:1-16) one of the central themes of the Scriptures is that we should love one another rather than hate one another, that we should forgive one another rather than condemn one another, and that we should do good to one another rather than do evil to one another. God has established some basic laws of right and wrong by which we should govern our relationships to one another. These basic laws have their roots in the holiness of God. The seriousness of doing wrong to others is that it violates the basic laws of right and wrong. In violating the basic laws of right and wrong, the wrongdoer adopts a pattern of life that is inconsistent with the nature of God. What we do to one another is evidence enough that there is something basically wrong between us and our God.

The person who violates the civil law is liable for arrest, trial, and punishment. The person who has violated God's laws of right and wrong also faces punishment. It is a position for which we are responsible and from which we cannot escape. Rescue is our only way out.

WHY HE DOES IT

It is never pleasant to consider the sins men do. At best, what we see is undesirable, degrading, and depersonalizing. The worst side of the picture is almost too repulsive and too horrible to contemplate. Yet, what we see when we look at the sins men do is no more than the tip of an iceberg. The real substance of what is there lies hidden from view. Even more serious than what we are doing to one another is the reason we do it.

PERSONAL LEARNING ACTIVITY 2

Study Mark 7:14-23. Then write a paragraph explaining what Jesus taught about the relationship between what a person does and that person's thoughts, feelings, and values.

The Root from Which the Fruit Is Grown

Any orchardist will tell you that the quality of the root stock cannot be overemphasized, because the quality of the fruit is determined by the root from which it is grown. Jesus used this fact to teach a spiritual truth. Our deeds are the fruit growing out of the thoughts and feelings within us (Luke 6:43-45). The heart is the battleground on which the contests are waged. The actions we see in our lives are no more than evidences of whether the battles were won or lost. The thief steals because he has first given his heart to greed. The adulterer violates the integrity of relationships because he has first given his heart to lust. The murderer kills because he has first given his heart to anger or hate.

Why does man do the sins that he does? Why do not our actions conform to God's divine law of right and wrong? Because inwardly our hearts do not conform to God's divine holiness. It has already been pointed out that the writers of the Scriptures used a variety of words to express the different aspects of sin. Many of these terms emphasized what a person felt or decided or thought. The real problem of sin is at the very center of our being. It has tainted and distorted the image of God within us. Those elements that make up the development of personality are affected. Man's sinfulness erupts from the inside and affects everything that man does.

Because there is both good and evil in every person, humanity appears to be in a state of contradiction. The evil within seems to be against the natural world, against fellowman, against inner self, and against God.

Expressions of this inner struggle are apparent in both character and behavior. In this condition man is not at peace within and is not able to understand his own desires. Consequently, gluttony, sexual perversion, and other sins are outward manifestations of what is wrong with man at the center of his being. Cain and Abel are one of the earliest illustrations of this contradiction in man. Although sons of the same parents, their personalities were different. They appear to have been in opposition to each other in spirit, in concerns, and in deeds. In the same way in the history of interpersonal relationships, nation has been set against nation, class against class, race against race, and like Cain and Abel, brother against brother.

Contradictory actions that concern the inner self are not new. The mind seeks sovereignty of the body, but the body revolts: "For the good that I wish, I do not do; but I practice the very evil that I do not wish" (Rom. 7:19, NASB). Man has difficulty controlling the mind-body relationships, and counteractions continually lead to actions in persons' lives that are contrary to God's law. However, the basic problem is that man's heart is in revolt against the demands of God's holiness. The nature of mankind as a sinner is the root of all the major human problems.

PERSONAL LEARNING ACTIVITY 3
Study the "New Testament Words for Sin" and the "Old Testament Words for Sin" charts. Note the aspect of sin emphasized by each word. Then read the references. Meditate on each passage and try to understand more fully its meaning by concentrating on the aspect of sin being emphasized.

The Self-perpetuating Pattern
Anything that perverts God's plan or purpose of life for humanity is sin. The Bible warns of sin's deceitful ability to pervert God's plan or purpose. The Bible records numerous instances that demonstrate how sin can and does do so. The root of sin is unbelief. Sin is doing one's own will rather than trusting God. One does not believe God means what he says; consequently, he relies on himself. One does not accept God's judgment; he wants to be his own judge. The root of sin then drives humanity deeper and deeper into the quicksand of helplessness.

This is the pattern. Man is defeated on the battlefield of the heart, and that defeat is manifested in life actions. This pattern is inevitable for every person. This realization awakens the person to the fact that his predicament is desperate. Depravity means that, given the power to choose, each person inevitably chooses to rebel against the demands of God's holiness. Moreover, the person is incapable of doing anything to change the forces he has set in motion in his life or to avoid the consequences of those forces. There must be help from some source outside the self. There must be a rescue from the basic sin that is the reason men do the things they do (Rom. 7:14 to 8:1).

WHERE IT IS ALL LEADING

Mankind needs rescue from what he is doing to himself and from the reason he is doing it. However, the most urgent reason rescue is needed is the result of what he is doing. Sin leaves its mark. The character and expression of sin are marked in every life. The result is the self-deluding power of sin working in the midst of personal experience. Sin begins to leave its mark at the time the person assents to sin in his life. The individual then continues in a pattern of self-defeat until he fails in the chief end of life and finally dies vanquished. Then in the life that is beyond this life, sin delivers its final mark: the death that is beyond death.

Where Sin Is Leading in This Life

The Old and New Testaments paint a true picture of what sin does to life. Sin never elevates but always lowers: "Being filled with all unrighteousness, wickedness, greed, malice; full of envy, murder, strife, deceit, malice; they are gossips" (Rom. 1:29, NASB). Sin never builds but always destroys: " 'Destruction and misery are in their paths' " (Rom. 3:16, NASB). Sin never comforts but brings sorrow and remorse: "I know my transgressions, and my sin is ever before me. Against Thee, Thee only, I have sinned, and done what is evil in Thy sight, so that Thou art justified when Thou dost speak, and blameless when Thou dost judge" (Ps. 51:3-4, NASB). Sin never brings light but always darkness: "In whose case the god of this world has blinded the minds of the unbelieving, that they might not see the light of the gospel of the glory of Christ, who is the image of God" (2 Cor. 4:4, NASB). Sin never frees but always binds: "His own iniquities will capture the wicked, and he will be held with the cords of his sin" (Prov. 5:22, NASB). Sin never guides but always leads astray: "There is a way which seems right to a man, but its end is the way of death" (Prov. 14:12, NASB). Sin never lifts burdens but always adds greater ones: " 'Woe to the rebellious children,' declares the Lord, 'Who execute a plan, but not Mine, and make an alliance, but not of My Spirit, in order to add sin to sin' " (Isa. 30:1, NASB). Sin never brings peace but always leaves a guilty conscience: "Poverty and shame will come to him who neglects discipline, but he who regards reproof will be honored" (Prov. 13:18, NASB). Sin never has a good influence on society, but always produces judgment: "The house of the wicked will be destroyed, but the tent of the upright will flourish" (Prov. 14:11, NASB). Sin takes away virtue and increases the power of temptation. Sin never produces eternal life but always brings eternal condemnation: " 'He who believes in Him is not judged; he who does not believe has been judged already, because he has not believed in the name of the only begotten Son of God' " (John 3:18, NASB).

The ugly consequences of sin are staggering. Such consequences produce guilt and cause unrest, bring bondage and cause weakness in one's powers, and bring enmity and place a barrier between God and humanity. Note some of the consequences experienced in this life.

Inner Consequences: Anguish

Christ taught of the inward consequences of sin. He said that they are primarily spiritual. Shakespeare said, "Conscience does make cowards of us all." See what happened to Peter when he denied Jesus. When he went away from the denial experience and was able to examine his own spirit, his conscience hurt him and he wept. See Judas when he betrayed Jesus. The years of relationship walking with Jesus gripped Judas' mind and drove him to suicide.

These examples are saying something special. Judgment is God's intolerance of that which destroys his purpose in the life of one he loves. Judgment rests upon anything that enslaves and destroys the best in a person.

External Consequences: Bondage and Suffering

Christ taught this truth. For example, the alcoholic is shackled to a force he cannot shake. He is bound to a circumstance from which he cannot free himself. His bondage destroys him, his personality, and his usefulness. Consider the addict and his drugs. He may insist he can be rid of the habit. Yet it chains his mind, fetters his emotions, and binds his body. Like the alcoholic, his bondage destroys his personality and his usefulness. The tragedy of bondage is increased by the fact that often the sinner destroys not only himself but also his relationship with others.

Another external consequence is the suffering of others. An alcoholic runs over an innocent child; a drug addict murders; a sensualist rapes; a robber steals and takes life's substance. In every case suffering takes place, but not because the person suffering has sinned. Sin often results in the suffering of innocent persons.

Separation from God

In the beginning man came under the curse of sin and was driven from the presence of God. When Adam and Eve had listened to the serpent and had eaten of the fruit, their disobedience was revealed by God himself. He pronounced specific judgment upon their sin and placed them under curse of enmity with the serpent, the pain of the human flesh, the curse of the earth, the uncertainty and bitterness that may be a part of toil, and the finality of death. "So He drove the man out" (Gen. 3:24, NASB).

Sin ruptures a person's relationship with God, and loss of fellowship with God is bitter. The most tragic thing a person can do is to break fellowship with God. The empty loneliness leaves only desperate separation. This is the essence of spiritual death—separation from God and, consequently, from all the benefits that derive from a relationship with him.

PERSONAL LEARNING ACTIVITY 4

Read carefully Romans 1:21-31. Verses 24, 26, and 28 say that "God gave them up" and "God gave them over." In each case God's judgment upon sin in this life is described. On a sheet of paper write how each of these verses describes God's judgment upon sin.

Where Sin Is Leading Beyond This Life

Sin and an unrestored fellowship with God bring forth an inevitable but eternal result. Separation of the individual from his God in this life bears fruit in the life that is beyond this life: judgment and eternal death.

Judgment and Final Guilt

The consequence of sin is judgment. Judgment upon sin often begins as the sinner sins. The person who allows sin to dominate his life will suffer the consequences. There really are no options. Sin binds us to the reality of God in our lives. We have violated the moral nature of God and the moral order of things that God created. We have sinned against the nature of God himself. Therefore, judgment is necessary. God's determinative pro-

WALLOWITCH

There is no other loneliness as deep or as tragic as separation from God.

nouncement is that one shall reap the final reward of sin. Beyond this life and in the next the endlessness of future punishment is staggering to the imagination.

The determinative future judgment is a place, as well as a state of being, which is hell. Hell indicates the awful fate of those who do not repent. Just as a person chooses separation from God in this life, the same choice shifts into the next. Eternal separation from God is finally hell.

For the sinner, the devastating finality of judgment is real and terrible. Guilt and responsibility are established by the proclamation of God himself.

Death

God's perfect justice demands punishment of sin. The Scriptures declare that the punishment is death: " 'But from the tree of the knowledge of good and evil you shall not eat, for in the day that you eat from it you shall surely die' " (Gen. 2:17, NASB). "For the wages of sin is death" (Rom. 6:23, NASB).

The consequences of sin are universal. Guilt and penalty go together. The chief penalty for guilt is death, physical and spiritual. The final issue of sin is death. The final harvest sin yields is death. Even though we overcome every other enemy, death finally overtakes us. God's justice made death the companion of sin. The seriousness of sin recognizes that the two are inseparable. The Scripture says, "The wages of sin is death" (Rom. 6:23, NASB).

Death is threefold: natural death, spiritual death, and eternal death. Natural death is a separation of the spirit from the body. Death has always been a natural law of the world, and the natural law of a human being finally separates the life from the body. Natural death is the event that marks the transition from this life to the next. Spiritual death is the separation of the spirit from God. It is a condition that exists in this life and is the result of a person's choosing to do those things that separate him from God. Yet, it is not a condition that cannot be changed. Eternal death is the complete and unending separation from God in the next life. It is characterized by the permanent, unchangeable, devastating absence of spiritual life and loss of fellowship with God.

Death, therefore—natural, spiritual, and eternal—is the product of sin: "Nevertheless death reigned from Adam until Moses, even over those who had not sinned in the likeness of Adam's offense, who is a type of Him who was to come" (Rom. 5:14, NASB). Every person must understand and recognize that the penal reality of death is real: "Therefore what benefit were you then deriving from the things of which you are now ashamed? For the outcome of those things is death" (Rom. 6:21, NASB). "For the mind set on the flesh is death, but the mind set on the Spirit is life and peace" (Rom. 8:6, NASB). "Then when lust has conceived, it gives birth to sin; and when sin is accomplished, it brings forth death" (Jas. 1:15, NASB).

CONCLUSION

What mankind is doing to himself (corruptive wrongdoing), why he is doing it (his inner inconsistency with the holiness of God), and where it is leading him (alienation from himself, from others, and from God, both now and eternally) point to one great truth. Mankind is in desperate need of help that he cannot give himself. That's the bad news.

The only hope for escape from judgment against sin and the sinner rests in God's initiative through Jesus Christ, his Son. This is the good news of Christ. The helplessness of the sinner can be dealt with if God deals with it through his provision of salvation. Humanity's needs can be settled only by the salvation God the Father provides. That's the good news that the next chapter deals with.

FOR FURTHER STUDY

Farley, Gary. *The Doctrine of God.* Nashville: Convention Press, 1977, chapters 3, 4.

Hendricks, William L. *The Doctrine of Man.* Nashville: Convention Press, 1977, chapters 1, 2, 6.

Grayum, H. Frank (ed.). *Bible Truths for Today.* Nashville: Convention Press, 1970, chapters 6, 7, 10.

Stagg, Frank. *New Testament Theology.* Nashville: Broadman Press, 1962, chapter 2.

Hobbs, Herschel H. *The Baptist Faith and Message.* Nashville: Convention Press, 1971.

Old Testament

Hebrew Word	Pronunciation	Literal Meaning
עָוָה AVAH	ăh-VĂH	commit iniquity, to bend or twist, distort, do wrong, to be perverted
שָׁגָה SHAGAH	shă-GĂH	go astray, to err, to wander, be deceived

NOTE: All Scripture references are taken from the Revised Standard Version, 1972 edition.

By Ronald W. Johnson

Words for Sin

Meanings and Examples from Old Testament Scriptures

This Hebrew word often describes the state of the sinner himself. The word also carries the idea of intentional wrong-doing.

1. The word describes a perverted mind. Example: "A man is commended according to his good sense, but one of perverse mind is despised" (Prov. 12:8).

2. The word carries the meaning also of a perversion of what is right. Example: " ' ". . . I sinned, and perverted what was right . . ." ' " (Job 33:27).

3. Another usage is that of iniquity. Example: " 'They have turned back to the iniquities of their forefathers . . .' " (Jer. 11:10).

Other examples: 1 Kings 8:47; 2 Chronicles 6:37; Lamentations 2:14; Ezekiel 4:7; Job 22:5; 1 Kings 17:18.

---

1. The word carries the basic idea of sin through ignorance. The picture is that of a sheep that wanders off from the fold. Example: " 'My sheep were scattered, they wandered over all the mountains and on every high hill . . .' " (Ezek. 34:6).

2. The word carries the idea of sinning in a moral sense. Example: " 'Teach me, and I will be silent; make me understand how I have erred' " (Job 6:24).

Other examples: Isaiah 28:7; Proverbs 20:1; Proverbs 5:23; Leviticus 4:13; Numbers 15:22.

רַע RA	RĂH	evil, bad, distress, misery, harm, ill favor, wickednes
חָמָס CHAMAS	hă-MĂS	do violence, violate, wrong damage

---

1. One of the most common forms for evil. It carries the idea of that which is in a sad state of affairs. It refers to moral and spiritual badness. Examples: "The soul of the wicked desires evil; his neighbor finds no mercy in his eyes" (Prov. 21:10).

". . . and said, 'I beg you, my brothers, do not act so wickedly' " (Gen. 19:7).

Other examples: Proverbs 25:19; Job 34:24; Isaiah 24:19; Isaiah 8:9.

---

1. The word can mean wrong done in the context of human relations. Example: " ' ". . . And do no wrong or violence to the alien, the fatherless, and the widow, nor shed innocent blood in this place" ' " (Jer. 22:3).

2. The word also can relate to ethical wrong. Examples: "Her prophets are wanton, faithless men; her priests profane what is sacred, they do violence to the law" (Zeph. 3:4).

3. "Now the earth was corrupt in God's sight, and the earth was filled with violence" (Gen. 6:11).

Other examples: Ezekiel 22:26; Lamentations 2:6; Job 15:33; Job 21:27; Proverbs 8:36.

חָטָא hă-TĂH to miss (a goal), be in fault, commit sin, have done harm, to go wrong

CHATA

מָאֵן mă-ĔN to refuse to obey

MAEN

---

1. Originally, the word carried the idea of being able to account for every possession. Example: " '. . . and you shall inspect your fold and miss nothing' " (Job 5:24).

2. The word's larger meaning indicates moral or spiritual failure. Example: "Then Pharaoh called Moses and Aaron in haste, and said, 'I have sinned against the Lord your God, and against you' " (Ex. 10:16).

Other examples: Exodus 32:33; Leviticus 4:3; Numbers 14:40; 1 Sam. 12:23; 1 Kings 8:47.

---

1. The word carries the idea of someone who refuses to honor a contract or promise. Example: " '. . . "My husband's brother refuses to perpetuate his brother's name in Israel; he will not perform the duty of a husband's brother to me" ' " (Deut. 25:7).

2. The word also can carry the idea of refusing to obey a command, especially from God. Example: "Then the Lord said to Moses, 'Pharaoh's heart is hardened, he refuses to let the people go' " (Ex. 7:14).

Other examples: Exodus 10:3; Exodus 16:28; Exodus 10:4; Nehemiah 9:17; Proverbs 21:7.

פָּשַׁע PASHA	pă-SHĂ	rebel, transgress, revolt, trespass
רָשַׁע RASHA	ră-SHĂ	be wicked, do wickedly, act wickedly, criminal, corrupt, guilty

In the Old Testament פֶּשַׁע is the most important word for sin as revolt against God.

1. One meaning of this word is that of rebellion or revolt on the part of a nation. Example: "So Israel has been in rebellion against the house of David to this day" (1 Kings 12:19).

2. Another meaning is transgression against God or rebellion against God. Example: ". . . for the ways of the Lord are right, and the upright walk in them, but transgressors stumble in them" (Hos. 14:9).

Other examples: 2 Kings 1:1; 2 Kings 3:5,7; 2 Chronicles 10:19; 2 Chronicles 21:8,10; Isaiah 1:28; Isaiah 46:8; Amos 4:4; Lamentations 3:42; Daniel 8:23.

---

1. This word means to behave wickedly. It indicates that the nature of the individual is corrupt. It is the exact opposite of the word which means righteous. It is used to describe an action which is ethically wrong. Example: " ' "We have sinned, and have acted perversely and wickedly" ' " (1 Kings 8:47).

2. The word can also carry the idea of being found guilty of one's sin. It can refer to guilt in human relations or in ethical or religious relations. Example: " ' . . . although thou knowest that I am not guilty . . . ' " (Job 10:7).

This word is also the Old Testament's most important word for sinner.

Other examples: Deuteronomy 25:1; Job 34:12; 2 Samuel 22:22; Job 9:29; Nehemiah 9:33; Daniel 12:10.

חָנֵף CHANEPH	hă-NĔF	be polluted, profane, godless, incline away from right, be defiled, corrupt
מָעַל MAAL	mă-ĂL	falsehood, transgression, to act treacherously, trespass, unfaithful

---

1. This word carries the idea of a violation of that which s supposed to be holy. It can apply to the land or to holy nen. Example: "The earth lies polluted under its inhabit-ants; for they have transgressed the laws, violated the stat-ites, broken the everlasting covenant" (Isa. 24:5).

2. It also can mean to become estranged from God. Ex-ample: " 'Both prophet and priest are ungodly; even in my iouse I have found their wickedness, says the Lord' " (Jer. 23:11).

Other examples: Jeremiah 3:1,9; Micah 4:11; Numbers 35:33; Daniel 11:32.

---

1. One usage of this word is in the husband-wife relation-hip. This usage deals with marital infidelity. Example: 'And when he has made her drink the water, then, if she ias defiled herself and has acted unfaithfully against her iusband . . .' " (Num. 5:27).

2. Another usage is in relationship with God. It can mean o act unfaithfully or treacherously against God. It refers to acrilege and apostasy from God. Example: "Behold, these aused the people of Israel, by the counsel of Balaam, to act reacherously against the Lord . . .' " (Num. 31:16).

Other examples: Deuteronomy 32:51; 1 Chronicles 5:25; Jehemiah 13:27; Ezekiel 39:23; Joshua 22:22.

New Testament

Greek Word	Pronunciation	Literal Meaning
ἀδικία ADIKIA	a-dĭ-KĒY-ŭh	unrighteousness, injustic[e] wickedness, wrongdoing
ἀνομία ANOMIA	ă-nō-MĒ-ŭh	lawlessness, defiance of law

Words for Sin

Meanings and Examples from New Testament Scriptures

1. The idea of a misdeed is present in the term. It refers to some wrong done to someone else. Example: " 'For I will be merciful toward their iniquities [misdeeds]' " (Heb. 8:12).

2. Another meaning has to do with injustice. Example: "What shall we say then? Is there injustice on God's part? . . ." (Rom. 9:14).

3. The term also carries the idea of wickedness and wrong against God. Example: "They were filled with all manner of wickedness, evil, covetousness, malice. . . ." (Rom. 1:29).

Other examples: 2 Corinthians 12:13; Romans 1:18; 1 Corinthians 13:6; 2 Peter 2:13.

This word is used of Satan and the antichrist.

1. The New Testament uses this term to describe a frame of mind of one who despises the law. Example: "Let no one deceive you in any way; for that day will not come, unless the rebellion comes first, and the man of lawlessness is revealed, the son of perdition" (2 Thess. 2:3).

2. The word can also be used to describe a lawless deed. Example: ". . . 'I will remember their sins and their misdeeds no more' " (Heb. 10:17).

Other examples: Romans 6:19; Hebrews 8:12; Matthew 24:12; 2 Corinthians 6:14.

ἁμαρτία hă-măr-TĒ-ŭh

HAMARTIA

to fail to hit the mark, a bad action, evil deed, offense, to sin against God, deceptive power

Most common term used in the New Testament to describe sin. It has several meanings and usages in the New Testament.

1. It is a departure from that which is right. Example: "All wrongdoing is sin, but there is sin which is not mortal" (1 John 5:17).

2. In the writings of John ἁμαρτία is described as a condition that is opposed to truth. It is an alienation from God. Example: "If we say we have no sin, we deceive ourselves, and the truth is not in us" (1 John 1:8).

3. Paul conceived of ἁμαρτία in personal terms; that is, he saw it as a ruling power the Christian must oppose. Paul also saw sin as a quality of life that is against God. Example: "Therefore as sin came into the world through one man and death through sin, and so death spread to all men because all men sinned" (Rom. 5:12).

4. In the book of Hebrews sin is seen as a power which can deceive men. Example: "But exhort one another every day, as long as it is called 'today,' that none of you may be hardened by the deceitfulness of sin" (Heb. 3:13).

Other examples: 1 Peter 4:8; 1 John 3:4; John 9:41; Romans 7:17; 1 Peter 3:18; Mark 2:5.

απιστία APISTIA	ă-pĭs-TĒ-ŭh	unfaithfulness, unbelief

ασέλγεια ASELGIA	ă-SĔL-ghĭ-ă	licentiousness, debauchery, sensuality, filthy

---

---

1. The primary meaning in the New Testament seems to be a lack of belief. It can be as strong as disbelief. Example: "And he did not do many mighty works there, because of their unbelief" (Matt. 13:58).

2. The word also carries the idea of unfaithfulness or the betrayal of a trust. Example: "What if some were unfaithful? Does their faithlessness nullify the faithfulness of God?" (Rom. 3:3).

Other examples: Hebrews 3:12; Mark 6:6; Mark 9:24; 1 Timothy 1:13.

This term is used to describe a baseness of life. It describes one who is in the total grip of sin and whose purpose in life is to satisfy desire. Example: ". . . they have become callous and have given themselves up to licentousness, greedy to practice every kind of uncleanness" (Eph. 4:19).

Other examples: Jude 4; 1 Peter 4:3; 2 Peter 2:2; Romans 13:13.

ἐπιθυμία ĕ-pĭ-thŏŏ-MĒ-ăh desire
EPITHUMIA

ἔχθρα ĔK-thră enmity, hatred
ECHTRA

The basic meaning of the word is desire. One must consult the context in order to see how the word is used. It can mean good or bad desire. Negatively it can mean several things.

1. It can mean a desire for other things (covetousness). Example: " '. . . but the cares of the world, and the delight in riches, and the desire for other things, enter in and choke the word, and it proves unfruitful' " (Mark 4:19).

2. It can be a desire for something forbidden as in lust. Example: ". . . and especially those who indulge in the lust of defiling passion and despise authority" (2 Pet. 2:10).

Other examples: James 1:14; 1 Thessalonians 4:5; Romans 13:14; John 8:44.

This term is generally used to describe a hatred or enmity against God. Example: "For the mind that is set on the flesh is hostile to God; . . ." (Rom. 8:7).

Other examples: James 4:4; Ephesians 2:14-16; Luke 23:12; Galatians 5:20.

ἀσέβεια ă-SĒĒ-bē-ăh godlessness, impiety

ASEBEIA

The idea of one who is ungodly is present in this word. It refers to those who progress further into godlessness. Example: “Avoid such godless chatter, for it will lead people into more and more ungodliness” (2 Tim. 2:16).

Other examples: Titus 2:12; Romans 1:18; Romans 11:26; Jude 18.

Κακία | kă-KĒY-ăh | depravity, malice, badness, wickedness

KAKIA

παράβασις | pă-RĂ-bă-sis | overstepping, transgression violation of law

PARABASIS

This term is a strong one in the New Testament. In the New Testament its main usage is to describe moral depravity or wickedness. Example: "Therefore put away all filthiness and rank growth of wickedness and receive with meekness the implanted word, which is able to save your souls" (Jas. 1:21).

Other examples: 1 Peter 2:16; Acts 8:22; 1 Corinthians 14:20; Hebrews 1:3.

This term refers to a wilful violation of the law. It also carries the idea of going beyond the limits or boundaries of the laws of God. Example: "For the law brings wrath, but where there is no law there is no transgression" (Rom. 4:15).

Other examples: Romans 2:23; Romans 4:15; Hebrews 9:15; 1 Timothy 2:14.

God's eternal purpose is to bring man home again to himself.

Chapter 2

Salvation: God's Eternal Purpose

Take an extended vacation trip without a plan? Not me. Perhaps I'll spread out the maps, talk it over with the family, and then work out my own plan. Or maybe I'll write an automobile association or one of the oil companies for a marked map. Whichever way I get the plan, it will take me from home to my final destination and back home again. Do you know that God had a plan before there were any roads or maps or even people?

Before the world began, God worked out a plan for every star, for every flower, for every animal, and for every person. Before God ever began creation, there was a plan for you, too. God has a purpose. This purpose was laid out carefully before creation began; it is the reason God has moved and has continued to move in the world as he does; and it is a purpose whose scope and reach encompass everything God has created.

WHAT IS GOD'S PURPOSE?

The purpose for planning my vacation trip was to get me where I wanted to go and to bring me home again. God made us for himself, and his great plan or purpose is to bring us home again to himself. Persons try to live without God, but that is not his purpose for them. We wander away from God's plan for our lives. We take many detours. We even try shortcuts. God is always calling us back to his eternal plan for us.

This is a general statement of a truth so vast that its many implications could never be explored fully. But if I were asked to say in one sweeping statement what God's purpose is, I would have to say it is to bring man home again to himself.

PERSONAL LEARNING ACTIVITY 5
Before continuing, think about God's eternal plan for the world and for you. Ask yourself these questions and try to arrive at a definite answer in your own mind.

1. **Do you think that God has a purpose and a plan for everything?**
2. **Does God force us to follow his plan for the world and for us?**
3. **Did God give us a road map that shows us the way to live in his purpose?**

In the beginning God began working out his purpose for humanity. God created the universe, the world, and humanity. In his creation God acted freely and without compulsion toward a moral and spiritual end. He communicated his own life and being to his own created beings. All that God created has purpose and meaning. It is not a hopeless riddle. God exercised control to express his dominion over everything that he created (Ps. 104:1-31). The remainder of this book will be an attempt to see how God moves to work out his eternal purpose and to see how working out that purpose affects the lives of persons.

HOW GOD'S PURPOSE HAS BEEN REVEALED

God wants humanity to be aware of his eternal purpose. The ways God has revealed or has reflected his eternal purpose are countless. This study will consider only three: God's will for the creation, God's moving in the history of Israel, and the incarnation of Christ.

Creation Reveals God's Eternal Purpose

No one can contemplate the splendor of God's creative glory without being impressed with his great activity in all the universe. The whole creation is an affirmation of the majesty of God. All nature speaks of God's sovereignty: "O Lord, our Lord, how majestic is Thy name in all the earth . . . . When I consider Thy heavens, the work of Thy fingers . . ." (Ps. 8:1-3, NASB).

God reveals himself to people through nature. He indwells the universe and all that he has created to show his power and authority. All nature and humanity depend on God's gift of life and sustenance. Paul said, "In Him all things were created, both in the heavens and on earth, visible and invisible . . . and in Him all things hold together" (Col. 1:16-17, NASB).

Through the world of nature, God shares his own nature and his will for peace and harmony in the world. The universe was planned to express his own glorious purpose of love and holiness. But because of man's sin, the creation's ability to reflect the glory of God has been dissipated. The state of nature seemed worse to Paul than the state of humanity because it was subjected to the voluntary act of sin on man's part. Without a choice nature was involved in sin's counterpurposes and suffered the consequences of sin. So the apostle told us this is a fallen world in which society's central condition is based on the nature of human frailty. Yet in it grows a deep longing for salvation when sin's dominion will be broken, when death and decay will be over. Nature awaits liberation from the sin that man brought into the world. "The creation was subjected to futility, not of its own will, but because of Him who subjected it, in hope that the creation itself also will be set free from its slavery to corruption into the freedom of the glory of the children of God" (Rom. 8:20-21, NASB). For him the ultimate purpose of nature in the world was to reveal his glory: "The anxious longing of the creation . . . for the revealing of the sons of God" (Rom. 8:19, NASB).

PERSONAL LEARNING ACTIVITY 6
Make a written list of all you think you see revealed in nature about God. Do you think you could have known these things about God, including his existence, if you had never had a Bible or any teaching about God from your parents, from the church, or from any other source? In the light of your answer, do you think someone could see and understand enough about God in nature to become a Christian?

The History of Israel Reveals God's Purpose
Everything God has done moves toward his goal. In the eternal struggle he consistently directed human affairs to his own pur-

poses.

Israel's history could be characterized by the hope for the time when the Creator's purpose would be realized: " 'Thus says the Lord, the King of Israel and his Redeemer, the Lord of hosts: "I am the first and I am the last, and there is no God besides Me" ' " (Isa. 44:6, NASB). "In Him all things were created, both in the heavens and on earth, visible and invisible, whether thrones or dominions or rulers or authorities—all things have been created through Him and for Him. So that He Himself might come to have first place in everything" (Col. 1:16,18, NASB).

God's purpose for the salvation of his world is seen in his relationship to Israel. He spoke to Abraham, the father of the Hebrew people, and disclosed the foundation for his moral kingdom: "Even so Abraham believed God, and it was reckoned to him as righteousness. Therefore, be sure that it is those who are of faith that are sons of Abraham" (Gal. 3:6-7, NASB). His redemptive purpose was laid and was tested in the long history of Israel.

God controlled that history. He used it, and he continues to use it, to help fulfill his purpose of salvation for humanity today. It is written of Israel: " 'All the nations shall be blessed in you.' So then those who are of faith are blessed with Abraham, the believer" (Gal. 3:8-9, NASB).

Israel was a special people. They were known as the "people of Yahweh." They were a special nation because their covenant relationship with God distinguished them from all other nations. Israel as a nation and the Jews as individuals were dependent on him who delivered and bound them to himself. God wanted his people to enjoy the blessings of his fellowship. No other people were so bound by covenant loyalty to him and to one another.

Israel was the nation of hope. Her religion was a religion of hope. God rescued them from slavery and led them from the wilderness trials to establish fully his covenant relationship with them. To Israel, God was the God who redeems. In the hope and history of Israel, we see the essence of God's purpose: to deliver and to save his people.

The Incarnation Reveals God's Eternal Purpose

History and theology both affirm that God has acted for the good of humanity. God's revealing himself to man reaches its climax in the coming of Christ our Lord into the world to provide for us and to offer to us salvation—the way back to God.

Christ is the expression of God's nature. The divine personality is expressed through Christ. He is the image of the invisible God and reflects God's own person and is his fullness: "He is the image of the invisible God, the firstborn of all creation. He is before all things, and in Him all things hold together" (Col. 1:15,17, NASB). "That they might not see the light of the gospel of the glory of Christ, who is the image of God" (2 Cor. 4:4, NASB). Christ is the supreme revelation of all that has ever been. He is without beginning and without end. He bears the stamp of God's nature, "and He is the radiance of His glory and the exact representation of His nature" (Heb. 1:3, NASB). It is in Christ that God's purpose is seen most clearly.

The basis for believing that he loves us is historical. Concern for us is from before the creation of the world. This is not reformation; it is recreation. The coming of his Son as the fullness of God is the real concern. For it was the Father's good pleasure for all the fullness to dwell in him. "In the beginning was the Word, and the Word was with God, and the Word was God. In Him was life; and the life was the light of men" (John 1:1,4, NASB). This is a redeeming work through the death of his Son for the saving of mankind. The divine agent in it was the Holy Spirit: "He saved us, not on the basis of deeds which we have done in righteousness, but according to His mercy, by the washing of regeneration and renewing by the Holy Spirit" (Titus 3:5, NASB).

God's final purpose for salvation not only is revealed but also is accomplished through his Son. The preparation for this was from the foundation of the world. The divine activity of it is in the beginning of creation: "In the beginning was the Word" (John 1:1, NASB). The Scriptures state that Jesus was the agent of creation: "For in Him all things were created" (Col. 1:16, NASB).

This is God's most significant invasion of human history. The coming of Christ was a divine act based on God's creative and covenant relationship with man. The covenant that God has made with man always reflects a personal relationship: " 'Behold, days are coming,' declares the Lord, 'when I will make a new covenant with the house of Israel and with the house of

Judah. . . . I will put My law within them, and on their heart I will write it . . . . "Know the Lord," for they shall all know Me, from the least of them to the greatest . . . for I will forgive their iniquity, and their sin I will remember no more' " (Jer. 31:31-34, NASB).

WHAT GOD'S PURPOSE MEANS TO MAN

At the center of everything God did was his purpose for humanity. Although the scope of his will includes nature and human history, God does will that nature glorify and reveal him, and he does purpose to redeem his creation. Also, God has acted, and continues to act, in human history. However, his ultimate purpose is salvation—bringing man home again to himself.

It Means Being Created Again

God's redemptive purpose, therefore, is the creation of a new humanity by making new persons. Humanity has great worth and value to God. God created mankind in his own image. Man is no afterthought with God. He is God's forethought, the crown of his creation. God completed his creation with human personality. Created a perfect being, a person was the highest attainment in the creation.

Persons were to reflect the image of God rationally, morally, emotionally. They were to possess a will and be free spiritual beings in God's image.

Then sin entered the picture, defeated humanity, and left us little more than broken images of our Creator.

Adam was made in the image of God. Yet Adam fell into sin and affected the whole human race. In the nature of human beings, something worthless and corrupt arises: " 'Even so, every good tree bears good fruit; but the rotten tree bears bad fruit' " (Matt. 7:17, NASB). What man is like now is quite a contrast to what God is like.

Man, like ancient Israel, has lost a sense of community. Humanity is impaired by sin just as it was in the time of Israel. The people preferred to go their own way. Consequently, they distorted the purpose for which they were created and providentially sustained. This can be laid to human frailty. Their disobedience caused their failure.

God is a God of holiness. His characteristics reveal loving-kindness; yet he is not without jealousy and wrath. Love and righteousness reflect his person. All these attributes were expressed in creation and in God's involvement with humanity. As holy God, he offers salvation to sinful, lost mankind: "Pursue peace with all men, and the sanctification without which no one will see the Lord. See to it that no one comes short of the grace of God" (Heb. 12:14-15, NASB). To live the life of God, we must have the nature of God. This is impossible except as the person's heart and life are created again by the new birth. At the same time, recognize the reality that God's holiness condemns sin. His grace desires to forgive it. Our sin was condemned on the cross. Our sin is forgiven because of Jesus' death on the cross.

It Means Living Responsibly

God summons humanity to practice righteousness toward himself and toward other human beings: "He has told you, O man, what is good; and what does the Lord require of you but to do justice, to love kindness, and to walk humbly with your God?" (Mic. 6:8, NASB). Our failure in responsibility is evidence that we have destroyed the image in which we are created. There is no wonder that the Scriptures indicate that this is a fallen world. What humanity has failed to realize is that persons are responsible to God—even for irresponsibility. And violation of the divine laws of God must be accounted for to the just and holy God. Judgment, therefore, stands clearly against evil.

Responsibility to God calls for godly conduct. Our decisions are linked to obedience and to life's meaning. The Old Testament sets the pattern for it: " 'See, I have set before you today life and prosperity, and death and adversity; in that I command you today to love the Lord your God, to walk in His ways and to keep His commandments and His statutes and His judgments, that you may live and multiply, and that the Lord your God may bless you in the land where you are entering to possess it' " (Deut. 30:15-16, NASB). The New Testament follows with the apostle Paul's admonition: "I, therefore, the prisoner of the Lord, entreat you to walk in a manner worthy of the calling with which you have been called, with all humility and gentleness, with patience, showing forbearance to one another in love, being diligent to preserve the unity of the Spirit in the bond of peace" (Eph. 4:1-3, NASB).

Every person is responsible to God and to fellow human beings for his personal conduct. We live under the control and the sovereignty of the holy God. We are responsible to him for our way of life. Human conduct and the quality of the lives persons live show that evil has corrupted our responsibility to live responsibly. Yet we are responsible. We have failed in our responsibility, but we are still responsible to God for that failure.

The unbeliever usually drifts through life hoping for the best. Such a person has no source of strength through which to deal with life's problems and perplexities. Consequently, the central condition of humanity demands salvation. It is in the redeemed relationship that a person has the basis and the resources for striving to make responsible decisions and for trying to live responsibly in relation to God and to others.

PERSONAL LEARNING ACTIVITY 7
Divide a sheet of paper into two columns. Label one "non-Christian" and the other "Christian." List under "non-Christian" four things for which you feel a person who is not a Christian is responsible to God. Do the same thing under "Christian."

It has been said often, "The more light, the more responsibility." Do you believe this statement is true? Look at Matthew 11:20-24. What does this Scripture passage seem to be saying?

It Means Reconciliation
The final purpose of God was directed to human reconciliation through Christ: "Through Him to reconcile all things to Himself, having made peace through the blood of His cross; through Him, I say, whether things on earth or things in heaven. And although you were formerly alienated and hostile in mind, engaged in evil deeds, yet He has now reconciled you in His fleshly body through death, in order to present you before Him holy and blameless and beyond reproach" (Col. 1:20-22, NASB). Salvation's initiative came from God in that he was in Christ reconciling the world to himself. The very life of God was the life of self-giving love. This is a revelation of God which Christ gives both in his living and in his teaching.

HOW GOD FULFILLS HIS PURPOSE

Salvation is fulfilling God's original purpose of creation to be bound to him as a family in love and that the world be made a fit home for his children to live in and fellowship with him and with one another. Consequently, a bridge had to be thrown over the abyss that separated a holy God and sinful humanity. God came to us so that we may come to him.

By Taking the Initiative to Deal with the Problem

Mankind's sin had destroyed his realization of fulfillment in divine fellowship and had diverted him from the divine purpose. Because humanity was alienated from God by sin, it was necessary for the holy God to deal with transgression. God's worldwide purpose of grace cannot take place without Christ's death on the cross. On the cross God's holiness and his love were united. Judgment was executed on sin which separates humanity from God. God's sovereign plan for humanity is understood only in the context of that saving relationship through the crucifixion. He took the initiative to save humanity.

Salvation arose out of the nature of the infinite holy God. Because God is God, he is characteristically holy and cannot tolerate sin. His wrath is his relation to sin. Yet his nature is not confined to this one strict attribute. The Bible speaks of the God who loves, of the grace he graciously gives, and of his faithfulness to his people. These descriptive phrases are involved significantly in his holiness which demands humanity be spared judgment against sin. Therefore, the Christ of God acted to make salvation possible. Divine love drew him to us and imparts his grace to us.

God provides atonement, the self-giving of God. The atoning work of God's Son, Jesus Christ, clearly indicates the universality of his love and the fullness of his grace. Grace is the love of God in action on behalf of sinful humanity: "In order that in the ages to come He might show the surpassing riches of His grace in kindness toward us in Christ Jesus. For by grace you have been saved through faith; and that not of yourselves, it is the gift of God" (Eph. 2:7-8, NASB).

God intended to restore and to lead humanity to a new fellowship with himself. He wanted mankind to have real communion with him. God's ultimate mission in Christ is to restore all things to himself. Humanity is called to a unique fellowship with the Creator involving obedience to his will. This can be fulfilled only through Christ who is the subjective ground for believing. God's love is experiential: "Hope does not disappoint, because the love of God has been poured out within our hearts through the Holy Spirit who was given to us" (Rom. 5:5, NASB). Only through his Spirit can such fellowship be made complete.

By Offering a Single Universal Solution to the Single Universal Problem

Salvation is universally available. Salvation is available to every person through God's saving grace. God determined that his glory be made real to all persons. His forgiveness and salvation are available to all who will respond to him in faith. When this happens, the believer discovers an ultimate joy in the divine loving plan and purpose. God's purpose for his people begins in salvation. He willed the restoration of holiness and beneficial help to his people in rededication and in fellowship. He always had in mind the personhood of every individual.

So God's call is to all people. It is universal. Those who would know and would find him discover that God is eternal love. He is the reconciling Savior. He is the God of peace who is found most fully in Christ. God's purpose is to save all mankind from destruction and from sin to himself and to the joy of a new dynamic and eternal life.

PERSONAL LEARNING ACTIVITY 8

The closing section of this chapter states several important concepts. These are listed below. Copy them on a sheet of paper and write brief statements telling what they mean to you.

1. God's holiness condemns sin. His grace desires to forgive it.
2. Grace is the love of God in action.
3. God's love is experiential.
4. God's call is to all people.

SUMMARY

God's purpose involves all his creation, but especially persons. That purpose is primarily to bring persons back into fellowship with himself. Since evil has defeated man's ability to act responsibly, God does act responsibly out of love. He takes the initiative to do what has to be done to bring man back to the God in whose image man was created and in whom man is intended to find completeness.

FOR FURTHER STUDY

Farley, Gary. *The Doctrine of God.* Nashville: Convention Press, 1977, chapters 3, 4.

Grayum, H. Frank (ed.). *Bible Truths for Today.* Nashville: Convention Press, 1970, chapter 2.

Hobbs, Herschel H. *The Baptist Faith and Message.* Nashville: Convention Press, 1971.

It was necessary that the Son do what he alone could do to free mankind from the guilt of sin and to reconcile all persons to God.

Chapter 3

Salvation: the Savior's Incarnate Mission

"I'm coming to help you!" I cried. I seized a rope hanging from a huge tree limb and swung into the water near my friend who was frantically calling for help. He grabbed my legs; and with the help of our other friends, I pulled him to the safety of the river bank.

My friends's cry was out of a real need. My action was in response to his cry. Chapter 1 showed man as he is now—victim of a need that he has no resources to meet. Chapter 2 showed how God anticipated and planned to meet man's need even before man was created. This chapter deals with the very act of rescue—the moment in which God plunged himself into our existence to bring us out safely to himself.

REDEMPTION'S WHY AND HOW

The Father took the initiative in sending the Son into the world. Love prompted him to do so. The evidence showed that all persons needed to be rescued, else they perish. The Son must do what he alone can do to free mankind from the guilt of sin and to reconcile all persons to God. So, God, in the person of the Son, has come into our world to provide for us the salvation we cannot secure for ourselves. And he has done it in a way that is beyond man's comprehension. In contrast to the animal sacrifices and rules and laws of man, God uniquely expressed his love through the cross. God, by his own act and independent of what man might do, became man's redeemer.

Love: the Why of Redemption

The crowning act in God's relation to man is the act of atonement. This act grows out of God's love, a fact that cannot be overemphasized. God does not love us because Christ came and died. The reverse is true. Christ came and died because God loves us. " 'God so loved the world, that He gave His only begotten Son. . .' " (John 3:16, NASB). "God demonstates His own love toward us, in that while we were yet sinners, Christ died for us" (Rom. 5:8, NASB).

To create the heavens and the earth caused God no anguish. Yet to take away the sin of the world cost him his only Son. The Bible declares that "He [God] made Him [Christ] who knew no sin to be sin on our behalf, that we might become the righteousness of God in Him" (2 Cor. 5:21, NASB). Jesus came into our existence; he came under the curse of sin; he submitted to the sentence of pain, shame, and death, which a divine holiness and justice must pronounce upon sin. By doing so, he made it possible for us to be delivered from that bondage and from that death. Providing redemption for us in this way required the full action of his love.

A part of Jesus' awareness of himself and of his mission was that he must die to free others from death and to secure life for them. He reached out to unite sinners with the Father and with one another. In his act of love he judged sin, pardoned guilt, renewed fellowship, and vanquished death. What a redemption this is; and what a love to bring it to pass!

The Cross: the How of Redemption

The fact that Christ came into the world reflects the extent of mankind's desperate need. Christ wanted to restore between persons and God a relationship that had been lost. The Scriptures explicitly declare that this could not have been accomplished apart from his death. Paul explained that Christ redeemed us from the curse of the law by becoming a curse for us (Gal. 3:13). The writer of Hebrews shows how the death of Christ achieved for sinners a cleansing and purifying that no other sacrifice could achieve (Heb. 9:1 to 10:13). The Revelation declares Christ to be the one who "released us from our sins by His blood" (Rev. 1:5, NASB).

PERSONAL LEARNING ACTIVITY 9
In a dictionary (preferably a Bible dictionary) look up *righteousness, faith, justify, redemption,* and *propitiation.* Then study Romans 3:10-28 and write a paragraph that answers the following questions.
1. **Why does every person need salvation?**
2. **Why can a person not save himself?**
3. **How is God able to declare the sinner to be righteous and still to be just in his dealing with sin?**
4. **The chief priests and scribes mockingly said of Jesus, " 'He saved others; He cannot save Himself' " (Mark 15:31, NASB). Yet in their mockery they unknowingly stated a very important truth. What is the truth they stated?**

The redemption God wrought through Christ is something he alone could accomplish. The matter is taken out of our hands. Salvation is not a personal achievement. As you worked through the preceding personal learning activity, you should have seen that the work of Christ is the ground of salvation. There is no exception to the rule that all have sinned and need to have a change effected in their standing before God. Therefore, God acted and dealt with sin in and through Christ. Through a faith relationship, persons may accept as a gift the righteousness and justification they could never have achieved through personal effort. God is able to do this and not violate the rules of justice in dealing with sin, because sin has been dealt with—not in the sinner declared righteous, but in Christ, the righteous one who knew no sin.

There was only one way to deal with sin. That was the cross. Only the Son of the Father could have come to this place. None but Christ could deal with the presence and the power of sin and bring forth atonement and righteousness for the sinner. This death was no mere martyrdom. It was a sacrifice for the sins of the human race. This was God's way of providing remission of sins, of restoring broken fellowship, and of producing a righteous people. Understanding this truth about the cross brings awareness of God's love in its infinite depth and goodness.

Examine more closely the cross event. The cross gives proof of sin's terrible destructive power and at the same time reveals justice and mercy. That moment in history when Christ came to die is the ultimate expression of God's redeeming action by which atonement for humanity was accomplished. In that action with all its finality, forgiveness was made possible for every person; sin was covered; life was made new. In the cross, the penalty for sin was paid. That transaction was God's forever judgment and forever forgiveness. Like a great rope, sin had knotted itself into a stranglehold about the neck of humanity. It took the cross to break the knot and liberate the sinner.

Quite simply, our salvation depends on what Christ did at the cross. His achievement makes possible for us a new relationship with God. He was able to bring about a reconciliation experience that restores humanity to fellowship with the Father, a fellowship that had been lost because of sin. The horror of the cross became the beautiful expression of God's love. That experience was not to win God's love, but to express it.

At last, the same God who had proclaimed salvation entered the realm of our existence and provided it. The individual sinner, helpless and painfully hopeless, has a way to the Father. This way has been made possible through Christ.

PERSONAL LEARNING ACTIVITY 10

Spend five minutes silently meditating on the cross. Visualize the crucifixion scene. Meditate on the meaning of the cross for you. Then try to express your feelings and thoughts in writing. Find one other person with whom you can share what you have written.

REDEMPTION'S REVELATION

Jesus who appeared in time existed before time. He was with God and then appeared among us. He appeared in the flesh and was the very nature of God. Exchanging the one existence for the other, he renounced his glory to enter into our poverty. He left eternity to enter history. He became the fullness of God the Father in human form. He became the incarnate Word.

The primary purpose of his incarnation addresses itself to the fact of man's spiritual death. He is the holy light that chases away the night of our sin. He is love in action that seeks to save the lost. The ultimate revelation of God's saving grace can be found in no other religion or person.

In the incarnation, Jesus' primary purpose was to reveal God's saving grace. However, he also revealed some other important truths about God and about himself.

He Revealed God's Thoughts and Feelings Toward Man

Christ became the Word; he has always been the Word; he is forever the Word: "In the beginning was the Word, and the Word was with God, and the Word was God" (John 1:1, NASB). Words give definition to thought and feeling. A word is the crystallization of a thought or feeling. When God brought salvation to humanity through Christ, it was his thought and feeling toward man being crystallized.

In the Bible, *Word* relates to the power of God to perform what he intends. The Word goes forth not as a form of speech but as the power of God to act. To say Jesus is the Word is to say he is the crystallization of God's thoughts, feelings, and intentions toward man. The Scriptures support this. Note Paul's description of Jesus: "He is the image of the invisible God, the first-born of all creation. He is also head of the body, the church; and He is the beginning, the first-born from the dead; so that He Himself might come to have first place in everything. For it was the Father's good pleasure for all the fulness to dwell in Him" (Col. 1:15,18-19, NASB).

Both of these passages indicate that in Christ God made himself known in the flesh. The absolute fact of his true being is stated in this miraculous merging of the human and the divine. The Son of God is the eternal essence of the Father.

He Revealed the Nature of God

In Christ, God really gave us the facts about himself. In every aspect of his relationship with man, Christ reflected perfectly the nature of the Father. John recorded that Jesus said to Philip one day, " 'He who has seen Me has seen the Father' " (John 14:9, NASB). Compare John's statement with Paul's description of Jesus as the sum total of all that is in God. "For in Him all the fulness of Deity dwells in bodily form" (Col. 2:9, NASB).

In Jesus dwelt the totality of God's wisdom, power, and love. Here was the absolute revelation of who God is and what he has come to do for humanity in a form which mankind could see and know and understand. No affirmation of God's person and his particular nature is more clear than in the life of Christ. What has been the distant, unknowable, invisible, and unreachable God has now come into human experience. No longer will God be a stranger. Now any person can know God through Christ. The fact of Christ, the greatest of all proofs of a completely satisfying God, proves to be an inexhaustible source of power, wisdom. and love. The evidence of God in Christ is his personality and character which are perfect reflections of God, the Father. Jesus' character was so unique that he could be identified as God without any sense of blasphemy. Christ consciously rose to the highest of all ideals and compels us to admit it. God's ideals are fully realized in him.

PERSONAL LEARNING ACTIVITY 11
Words are the means by which persons identify objects, animals, birds, flowers, ideas, concepts, actions, and attitudes. Jesus Christ is the Word about God. Take a few minutes to think about the life of Jesus Christ. What words do you think of that identify the character, actions, and attitudes of God when you see *Jesus Christ?* After thinking about this, make a list of the single words that you apply to God when you see *Jesus Christ.* Now think about this: Do you think that these words about the Word are worth sharing with your family, your friends, and your neighbors?

He Revealed His Own Uniqueness
John proclaimed: "The Word became flesh, and dwelt among us, and we beheld His glory, glory as of the only begotten from the Father, full of grace and truth" (John 1:14, NASB). The overwhelming thrust of this statement is that the full glory of his own Godness is proof of his uniqueness. The wonder of who he is is staggering, yet real. Jesus' uniqueness is described by the Hebrews writer when he said: "He is the radiance of His glory and the exact representation of His nature, and upholds all things by the word of His power. When He had made purification of sins,

He sat down at the right hand of the Majesty on high; having become as much better than the angels, as He has inherited a more excellent name than they" (Heb. 1:3-4, NASB).

In the context of the above Scripture passage, the writer declared that Jesus is heir of all things. He created the universe. He is the shining radiance of God's glory and the full visible expression of the essence of the Father. He holds together the universe and is the one who died for our sins. He is presently seated at the right hand in a place of authority with the Father.

This same theme appears in Hebrews and in the writings of John and Paul. The uniqueness of Jesus' incarnate glory is revealed clearly in his teachings, in his ministry, in his death, in his resurrection, and in his ascension. He is presently at the right hand of the Father. His glorious advent is sure. Jesus Christ is the only person in history in whom God finds us and through whom we find God. That is good news. Good news is what Christ does universally. The secret of all the ages has burst into the human situation and is revealed in Christ (Eph. 2:3-13).

He Revealed the Meaning of Grace

Let us examine some of the phrases in John 1:14. The first phrase is "full of grace." God's attitude toward humanity is one of grace. He is the God of grace who is interested in the lives of all persons. He is loving and compassionate—not the stern, unforgiving, or legalistic God that some persons believe him to be. He is the supreme God of redeeming grace through his Son, Jesus Christ. The ultimate manifestation of grace for human salvation is simply stated. *He cared for us* is the meaning of the word *grace.* Grace means something undeserved and unmerited, something not earned or achieved. The word explains mankind's poverty and the limitless kindness of God's love. God's action, prompted by his love, bears out this fact.

God's righteous love beautifully expressed in his Son, the sinless one, tells us that salvation has come to the whole world through the great act of his eternal mercy. The fate of the whole world rests on this truth. This great act of love toward a hostile world is free and unmerited. Look at Christ on the cross and you discover the love of God. His holy love, intensely opposed to sin, has reached out to sinful humanity. No more meaningful expression can be found than when Jesus gave expression to the love of his Father. Jesus expressed the same love his Father expressed. He exemplified the same compassion that springs out of the very being of the Father's nature.

All persons are the objects of that love. For them Christ dared to die. He showed his love by submitting to death for sinners who are unattractive and undeserving. To say that Christ is "full of grace" is to say that he is filled with the irresistible desire to exercise love and mercy and faithfulness. Because of his limitless generosity, Christ does exercise love and mercy and faithfulness. And he does so far in excess of what persons deserve. It is in the grace of Christ that we are able to see what it means to say that God is Father. It is grace that revealed his spirit and his love. And it is his spirit and his love that enable us to believe that God is Father. It is his grace that enables persons to trust themselves absolutely to his forgiving love.

He Revealed the Ultimate Truth

In John 1:14 Jesus is said to be "full of truth" also. John 14 states that he embodied truth: "Jesus said to him, 'I am the way, and the truth, and the life; no one comes to the Father, but through Me' " (John 14:6, NASB). Jesus communicates truth. "Jesus therefore was saying to those Jews who had believed Him, 'If you abide in My word, then you are truly disciples of Mine; and you shall know the truth, and the truth shall make you free' " (John 8:31-32, NASB). Jesus guides into truth, and it makes one free: " 'The truth shall make you free' " (John 8:32, NASB).

Jesus lived as a man, subjected to the Father and limited in knowledge and in power. Yet he found all-sufficient resources in God to accomplish his will. By doing so, he related the truth of humanity's being and the truth of God's being to each other.

The history of Jesus and the history of personal salvation are clear. In ages past, God spoke to men and women through the prophets. Many of those spoken revelations were preparatory. Now his great truth has burst on the human mind and into the human situation. The facts of the Lord's life are truths for human inner life. The wellsprings of hope have broken forth to quench the parched land of withered mankind. Paul declared: "By common confession great is the mystery of godliness: He who was revealed in the flesh, was vindicated in the Spirit, beheld by angels, proclaimed among the nations, believed on in the world, taken up in glory" (1 Tim. 3:16, NASB). No other has spoken greater truths. No greater dynamic truth is made so real. Yet Christ became the deed of truth.

The truth of Christ's message is the truth of his action. So unique is the fact that he came to die, Peter exclaimed, "Christ also died for sins once for all, the just for the unjust, in order that He might bring us to God, having been put to death in the flesh, but made alive in the spirit" (1 Pet. 3:18, NASB). What an expression of the uniqueness of this sinlessness: the sinless for the unjust.

PERSONAL LEARNING ACTIVITY 12
This chapter has described Jesus as being "full of grace and truth." Another way to say that is to say that he is "the fullness" of grace and truth. In what ways is Jesus Christ "the fullness of grace"? Remember that grace is "unmerited favor." In what ways is Jesus Christ "the fullness of truth"?

REDEMPTION AND RESURRECTION

On the cross, Christ bore sin's penalty. This act was acceptable to God, and it was sufficient for our salvation. The seal and guarantee of this was the resurrection. The message is clear. The acts and sayings or teachings of Jesus point beyond the cross to the resurrection. Jesus died for sin. The resurrection was the way through death to the victory over sin. Paul pointed out this truth when he described Christ as the one "who was delivered up because of our transgressions, and was raised because of our justification" (Rom. 4:25, NASB).

Jesus approached the experience deliberately, yielding his life up to death. The Father gave it back to him in resurrection. Every person's hope of relationship to him can be found in that symbolic act. A person who yields his life to God in Christ is rewarded in love with a new life that is eternal, emphatic, dynamic, and complete.

Resurrection Defeats Sin and Death

Redemption defeats sin by the resurrection. Read 1 Corinthians

15. Sin can no longer threaten to sever the soul from God. No more can the law annihilate the sinner with condemnation and despair.

Death's mythical power and invincibility is shattered by God's victory in Christ. Jesus is the hope of salvation. The new age has arrived. Christ, as risen Lord, achieved the fullness of his true nature. He is no longer man in weakness; he is God in power. He fulfilled in his person the purpose of God. He entered the conflict of sin and death and won hope on behalf of humanity.

Resurrection Is New Life

The Son of God realized complete and ultimate victory over sin and death. Why? Because resurrection tells of new life. Paul indicated that a person can share Christ's risen life when he said, "That I may know Him, and the power of His resurrection and the fellowship of His sufferings, being conformed to His death; in order that I may attain to the resurrection from the dead" (Phil. 3:10-11, NASB). The believer depends on resurrection for the fullness of that new life. On the cross Christ bore the sin; in the resurrection he became victor over sin and death.

The miracle of new life is made sure in the risen Christ. If he is not risen, then he is bound to the limits of the natural. Some have called Christianity a product of the natural intellect. This is not true. It was God who brought Christ through death by giving him new life in the resurrection. It was by God's act that new life came to be and is made available to every person who will accept it.

Resurrection made secure the source of eternal life through faith. We depend on it, and we are united to him through it. It is by the power of the resurrected Christ that persons are able to become new beings.

CONCLUSION: CHRIST IS THE GOSPEL

The fact of salvation is a declaration that it is not hopeless to try to change the world. We cannot say that the world and society are so bad that nothing can be done about their condition. God's action in providing redemption gives an optimistic hope that leaves no room for such pessimism. Through Christ and what he has done for humanity, persons can live above the plane of human limitations. This is great news.

The gospel is the instrument God uses to bring about the desired end. The proclamation of good news is that salvation comes by Jesus Christ, God's Son, at every point in all relations. He is the Savior and the reconciling agent in every person's relationship with the Father. When humanity is estranged from God, Christ provides the means for alienation to be removed. The gospel proclaims Christ did something for us that we could not do for ourselves. In him every soul can find rest and every mourner can find peace and comfort.

Jesus Christ accomplished the task he was sent to earth to do. He completed a once-for-all offering for sin. He severed the cords of sin that bound humanity to the judgment of death. He stepped through the halls of death and turned darkness into light. For all people he sat down on the right hand of the Father as the absolute victor. He shall raise his scepter to reign and to rule forever.

Believing in or not believing in Jesus Christ for salvation decides each person's eternal destiny. The eternal decision rests with each individual. Jesus is the Word. He is the deed. The very God, the Word of truth, is life for all who will accept it. This is the gospel. This is salvation, for Christ is the Savior.

PERSONAL LEARNING ACTIVITY 13
On a sheet of paper make a list of things that Jesus Christ saves you from. Now make a list of the things that Jesus Christ has saved you to.

FOR FURTHER STUDY

Grayum, H. Frank (ed.). *Bible Truths for Today.* Nashville: Convention Press, 1970, chapter 3.

Stagg, Frank. *New Testament Theology.* Nashville: Broadman Press, 1962, chapter 3.

Hobbs, Herschel H. *The Baptist Faith and Message.* Nashville: Convention Press, 1971.

CLYDE DENTON, JR.

The Holy Spirit enables us to depend on the Father and causes the beauty of Christ and the joy of salvation to radiate from within the believer.

Chapter 4

Salvation: the Holy Spirit's Enabling Action

Oxygen is the breath of life. Astronauts must take it for their orbital voyages. In emergency medical units, doctors and nurses work fervently over victims to remove noxious gases from lungs and replace them with life-giving oxygen. When a drowning victim is dragged from death-gripping waters, emergency measures are taken to get oxygen into his lungs.

Oxygen is essential to sustaining body functions. Just as that life-giving gas is distributed into the bloodstream bringing life, so the "breath" of God is essential to the salvation of a person in God's divine plan revealed in Christ Jesus. The "breath" is the Holy Spirit. That is how he gets his name: "the Holy Breath," "Wind" of God.

There is evidence of the presence of the Holy Spirit from the beginning of biblical history. The Genesis account of creation records that "the Spirit of God was moving over the surface of the waters" (Gen. 1:2, NASB). The Old Testament uses many expressions to describe the presence, the power, and the work of the Holy Spirit. Christ spoke of the Spirit and promised his disciples that the Spirit would come to be with them permanently. Then the promise of Christ was fulfilled at Pentecost. The Holy Spirit is God operating in the world and in the lives of his believers.

This chapter will show how the Holy Spirit is the enabling agent in salvation. We shall see how he is, indeed, God's breath of eternal life. He is the one who enables sinners to come to the Savior. He is the one who breaks the bonds of spiritual death and imparts eternal life. He is the one who effects the continuing work of salvation in the life of the believer.

THE HOLY SPIRIT BRINGS THE SINNER TO SALVATION

It is a mistake to believe that the Holy Spirit operates only in the lives of believers. If it were not for the work of the Holy Spirit in the lives of unbelievers, no person would ever find salvation. The Scriptures speak plainly about man's spiritual blindness and insensitivity to the true nature of his condition (Rom. 2; Eph. 4:17-18). If left alone, man not only would remain separated from God; he would not even be aware of the separation.

PERSONAL LEARNING ACTIVITY 14
Before continuing the study, read John 15:18-27; 16:7-11. Then decide for yourself: Does the Holy Spirit work in the lives of unbelievers? If so, what does he do and for what purpose?

He Enables the Sinner to See His Need

The Holy Spirit is the messenger of the Father who comes to the sinner in the name of the Son. He speaks God's secrets and opens God's truths to hearts that otherwise would never have heard them. The gospel is the whole truth. This truth about Christ and what he has done is the good news to all people. By it, God reveals man's desperate condition and shows what must be done to remedy it. Truth shows us how sorely we need the salvation offered us by the grace of God. To deliver the message, the Holy Spirit deals with every element of personhood—the intellect, the emotions, the conscience, and the will. Whatever he does and however he wishes to do it, the Holy Spirit brings to bear on the consciousness of the individual Jesus Christ as God's truth. He does this so persuasively that the truth cannot be denied or ignored.

The term the Scriptures use to describe this convincing, undeniable presentation of truth is *convict.* " 'He, when He comes, will convict the world concerning sin, and righteousness, and judgment; concerning sin, because they do not believe in Me; and concerning righteousness, because I go to the Father, and you no longer behold Me; and concerning judgment, because the ruler of this world has been judged' " (John 16:8-11, NASB). His work related to sin and righteousness and judgment are not three works but three phases of the one work of conviction. The word *convict* is the intellectual and emotional penetration of the conscience. He probes the mind and the heart of an individual to bring an uneasy but inescapable understanding of one's true condition.

He Convicts of Sin

The Holy Spirit uses hearing the gospel as a means of conviction and opens the heart to the mystery of God's holy love. He directs attention to humanity condemned before God, not simply because they are sinners but because they have refused to believe the Savior and to accept his pardon. The Holy Spirit awakens in a person a sense of guilt and condemnation by causing sin to be understood in terms of unbelief. He confronts the sinner with the reality of personal sin. He produces a consciousness of guilt and a realization of condemnation. This is conviction of sin. The Holy Spirit shows that sin springs from unbelief, which is rejection of God in Christ.

He Convicts of Righteousness

The Holy Spirit convicts of righteousness: " 'He, when He comes, will convict the world concerning sin, and righteousness, and judgment; . . . and concerning righteousness, because I go to the Father, and you no longer behold Me' " (John 16:8-10, NASB). Righteousness is the essence of God's being. It is the opposite of sin. Righteousness is clearly revealed in the character and work of Christ. When Christ is brought to bear on the life of a person, his divinity, holiness, and righteousness uncover unholiness and unrighteousness.

The Holy Spirit compares the nature of Christ to human nature, thereby revealing the nature of sin. One cannot come in contact with God without being convinced of the righteous nature of Jesus and his own need for righteousness. Evil has invaded and penetrated one's whole being. The conscience, will, thoughts, and reasons are ensnared. The Holy Spirit makes the sinner aware that what he is is the opposite of what God is, and something needs to be done about it. The Spirit provides a thirst for salvation. He whets the appetite for wholeness which God alone can provide.

The Spirit works as the enlightening one in the life of the

individual. He lays bare the awareness of lostness. Lostness brings hopelessness. No wonder the jailer cried to Paul, " 'What must I do to be saved?' " (Acts 16:30, NASB). The probing, searching, moving, convicting power of God's Spirit was the only force that could evoke such a cry.

He Convicts of Judgment

The Holy Spirit convicts of judgment: " 'He, when He comes, will convict the world concerning sin, and righteousness, and judgment; . . . and concerning judgment, because the ruler of this world has been judged' " (John 16:8-11, NASB). God not only convinces persons of their sinfulness and their need for righteousness; he also convinces them that it is not necessary that they remain unrighteous and bound to the power and the penalty of sin. He convinces them that they can come away from sin, because sin has been judged.

Christ had laid bare the evil one's diabolical character. In the cross, Satan was judged and sentenced to total defeat. The Holy Spirit persuades sinners that because Satan's power was broken at the cross, it can be broken in their lives. However, he also warns of what will happen to those who persist in unbelief. Just as Satan is judged, so will be those who follow him, serve him, and submit to him. Judgment is certain for the person who withstands the conviction of the Holy Spirit and rejects Christ. " 'Then He will also say to those on His left, "Depart from Me, accursed ones, into eternal fire which has been prepared for the devil and his angels" ' " (Matt. 25:41, NASB).

He Enables the Sinner to See the Savior

Becoming aware of one's need is only a part of all that is involved in salvation. We have seen how the Holy Spirit, with a persuasive power, probes the heart and creates an awareness of need. However, an awareness of need is not enough to make salvation possible. Remember, the sinner is described as ignorant of the truth, hardened against the truth, and insensitive to the truth (Rom. 2; Eph. 4:17-18). The sinner has no awareness of his need until the Holy Spirit creates that awareness. Likewise, he has no idea what to do about the need until the Spirit reveals the Savior. Once when Jesus was talking to the disciples about the Spirit, he said, " 'When the Helper comes, whom I will send to you from the Father, . . . He will bear witness of Me' " (John 15:26, NASB). After the Spirit has persuaded the sinner that he needs to be rescued, he persuasively introduces Christ as the only hope.

He Brings the Sinner Out of Death to Life

The Holy Spirit calls to the spirit of a person and produces an awareness of sin. He brings Christ to bear upon the life and exposes unbelief. Then the sinner responds. In that moment of response is the moment of transformation—the moment of beginning. This is the moment in which the sinner moves from darkness into light. This is the moment when he is freed from spiritual death and raised to life in Christ.

This transformation is one that takes place only by the intervention of superior strength and goodness. The sinner has no inner resources or strength to bring it to pass. A miraculous change, a new act of creation takes place. A new being is called into existence. The Holy Spirit acts again with enabling power. He brings the new birth to pass. He is the one who breathes the spiritual breath of life into those who are spiritually dead. In his conversation with Nicodemus, Jesus said, " 'Truly, truly, I say to you, unless one is born of water and the Spirit, he cannot enter into the kingdom of God. That which is born of the flesh is flesh; and that which is born of the Spirit is spirit' " (John 3:5-6, NASB). In his letter to Titus, Paul referred to "the washing of regeneration and renewing by the Holy Spirit" (Titus 3:5, NASB). Both of these passages show that the Holy Spirit is the enabling agent in the miracle of regeneration.

THE HOLY SPIRIT CONTINUES THE WORK OF SALVATION IN THE BELIEVER

Christ said to his believers, " 'You are to be perfect, as your heavenly Father is perfect' " (Matt. 5:48, NASB). This is God's will for man. This is the reason that Christ came and died. This is the reason that the Holy Spirit works in the hearts of persons. God wants man to be as innocent, as perfect, and as righteous as when man was first created. The thirst for this holiness and righteousness is the desire kindled in the heart of the unbeliever by the Holy Spirit. To attain this holiness and righteousness is the reason the unbeliever acts in faith and trusts himself to God through Christ.

The new Christian soon discovers that the moment of faith in which regeneration takes place is not the end to which the Holy Spirit has been leading. It is only the beginning. The new believer discovers that the new birth does not put an end to sin in his life. It does not provide an easy solution to all of life's agonies. And it does not completely satisfy his heart's thirsting to be like God. The new believer discovers that he has by no means arrived at the end toward which the Holy Spirit has been leading. Instead, he has only begun a long journey that will lead him into Godlikeness. The Scriptures speak of this process as putting off the old man and putting on the new man as you would take off one coat and put on another (Col. 3:9-10; Eph. 4:22-24). It is described also as becoming unblamable in holiness before God (1 Thess. 3:13) and as becoming a perfect man in the fullness of Christ's stature (Eph. 4:13). The term most commonly used today to describe this process of becoming more and more like God is *sanctify* or *sanctification.*

PERSONAL LEARNING ACTIVITY 15
Use a dictionary to study the meanings of *sanctify* and *sanctification.* (Use a Bible dictionary if possible.) Then use a concordance to locate and read New Testament passages that contain these words.

Sanctification does not take place in the person's life without struggle. In addition to the phrases already mentioned, sanctification also is described as running a race, striving, fighting, and bringing one's body into subjection (1 Cor. 10:24-27). It is spoken of as self-denial and crossbearing (Matt. 16:24). Other passages describe sanctification with such extreme terms as self-crucifixion (Gal. 5:24; 2:20). Sanctification is not only a long journey; it is a demanding one. It is a journey we could neither begin nor complete without the enabling work of the Holy Spirit.

Presence
In the moment of faith, the Holy Spirit brings the believer from spiritual death into life. The believer is delivered from the con-

demnation of sin and made to share in the righteousness of God. But sin is still an ever present reality in the life of the believer. Satan does all in his power to keep the believer from becoming unblamable in holiness before God or from becoming a perfect man in the fullness of Christ's stature.

Christ was aware of the immense struggle his believers would face, so he promised them a helper. Jesus said: " 'I will ask the Father, and He will give you another Helper, that He may be with you forever; . . . but you know Him because He abides with you, and will be in you. I will not leave you as orphans; I will come to you' " (John 14:16-18, NASB).

From the moment one first believes, the Holy Spirit dwells in him and with him for all his journey into Godlikeness. He is the divine helper—the enabler. He puts courage in the life of the believer. He strengthens the believer to face adversity and gives hope in the midst of trial. The presence of the Holy Spirit is the inexhaustible source of power and assurance for the believer.

Power

When the Holy Spirit enters the life of a believer, he enters with enabling power. A part of the futility of being separated from Christ is the unbeliever's complete lack of power. The unbeliever has absolutely no inner resources to use to deal with the desperateness of his spiritual condition. He finds himself powerless to change his inclination to sin and powerless to resist sin's attraction. Through the ministry of the Holy Spirit, the power of sin and death is broken. "The law of the Spirit of life in Christ Jesus has set you free from the law of sin and of death" (Rom. 8:2, NASB).

Assurance

The Holy Spirit enables us to live with confidence even in life's darkest hours. The Father knows that the demands of the Christian life are extreme. He knows that the struggle to walk in the way of the Spirit tests his followers to the limit of their faith and endurance. So he does not leave us without solid assurances to sustain us in the darkest hours. We are enabled by the Holy Spirit. The New Testament uses at least three figures to describe the assurance the Holy Spirit gives the believer.

The Hope of Adoption

The Spirit assures us that we are children of God. "You have not received a spirit of slavery leading to fear again, but you have received a spirit of adoption as sons by which we cry out, 'Abba! Father!' The Spirit Himself bears witness with our spirit that we are children of God, and if children, heirs also, heirs of God and fellow-heirs with Christ, if indeed we suffer with Him in order that we may also be glorified with Him" (Rom. 8:15-17, NASB).

The Seal of Promise

The Holy Spirit is the seal of promise for the believer. "To the end that we who were the first to hope in Christ should be to the praise of His glory. In Him, you also, after listening to the message of truth, the gospel of your salvation—having also believed, you were sealed in Him with the Holy Spirit of promise" (Eph. 1:12-13, NASB). And he expresses the seal of ownership: "Nevertheless, the firm foundation of God stands, having this seal, 'The Lord knows those who are His' " (2 Tim. 2:19, NASB). In New Testament times, a seal indicated ownership. The Holy Spirit's indwelling the life of the believer is the seal and sign that indicates that the believer belongs to God.

In New Testament times, the seal was a token of a completed transaction. When an agreement was concluded and the price was paid, the seal was appended to the contract to make it secure. The seal also authenticated that which was genuine. The Holy Spirit in our lives denotes that the price has been paid and that God owns us genuinely and securely.

God's divine stamp on the believer indicates that the believer belongs to God. This stamp is the assurance imparted by the Holy Spirit to the new Christian that he is saved and is chosen for the day of glory when the final day of salvation is completed. The seal of promise declares that we belong to God forever.

The Earnest

The Holy Spirit guarantees the "earnest," God's pledge and token to all he promised in that relationship of salvation. "Who is given as a pledge of our inheritance, with a view to the redemption of God's own possession, to the praise of His glory" (Eph. 1:14, NASB). Earnest money is part of the purchase price paid in advance as a guarantee that the rest of the price will be paid when due. God's guarantee is that someday every believer will enter into the fullness of his knowledge, of his power, and of his glory. The guarantee is that full redemption is true and that we shall receive its benefits forever. One may believe with certainty and in great joy that God has made the first and final installment for our salvation. "Now He who establishes us with you in Christ and anointed us in God, who also sealed us and gave us the Spirit in our hearts as a pledge" (2 Cor. 1:21-22, NASB).

PERSONAL LEARNING ACTIVITY 16

Some of the following phrases are related to the work of the Holy Spirit and some are not. Without rereading the chapter, underline those phrases that are related to the Holy Spirit: reveals Christ, makes us intelligent, born of the Spirit, sanctifies us, sets us free, purifies us, makes us prosperous, helps us love one another, keeps us healthy, seals us in Christ, is the earnest of our inheritance. Write brief explanations of the phrases that you have underlined.

SUMMARY

Humanity flounders in darkness and has no ability to solve any of the truly essential problems of human nature. Only the Holy One can solve them. The Holy Spirit does it by breathing new life into everyone who will commit himself to Christ in faith. He will accomplish salvation fully in due time. He teaches the truths that cannot be understood by the world. He is the one who gives life. It is he who gives us understanding. He enables us both to depend on the Father and to live in the full bloom of the blessings of his promises. The Holy Spirit makes Christ real and accomplishes the fullness of salvation.

FOR FURTHER STUDY

Hendricks, William L. *The Doctrine of Man.* Nashville: Convention Press, 1977, chapter 7.

Grayum, H. Frank (ed.). *Bible Truths for Today.* Nashville: Convention Press, 1970, chapter 4.

Hobbs, Herschel H. *The Baptist Faith and Message.* Nashville: Convention Press, 1971.

Salvation is based on God's initiative, not man's. God initiates contact with the person, and the person responds.

Chapter 5

Salvation: God's Action/Man's Response

Salvation is one of the most needed and the least sought after things in the universe. As the most valuable of all possessions, it is the least prized. Of all the possible acquisitions of life, salvation costs the most to provide but can be obtained free of charge. It is highly spoken of by God and available to all persons; but men regard it lightly, and few accept it.

Throughout the centuries humanity has attempted in many ways to find a right relationship with God. In ancient Greece and Rome philosophers reasoned, and states enacted their laws. The pagan world had its sacrificial rites and ceremonies. In all ages various religions have evolved because of man's search for God.

The history of salvation is like a stream flowing through the ages. The promise of salvation rose in the ancient times of the Old Testament through its heroes and its prophets. People of the Old Testament waited in faith for Messiah. The promise flowed onward through Bethlehem to Golgotha. Christ became the realization of their hopes and the fulfillment of prophecy. He became forever the Savior and Lord of all who would trust him.

The prophets of the Old Testament not only looked forward to Christ's coming, but they also explained the reason for his coming: "He was pierced through for our transgressions, He was crushed for our iniquities; the chastening for our well-being fell upon Him, and by His scourging we are healed. All of us like sheep have gone astray, each of us has turned to his own way; but the Lord has caused the iniquity of us all to fall on Him" (Isa. 53:5-6, NASB).

Then Christ came just as the prophets had said he would. He defeated the power of evil and conquered death. He gave forgiveness and life to those who would believe him and follow him. "He made Him who knew no sin to be sin on our behalf, that we might become the righteousness of God in Him" (2 Cor. 5:21, NASB); "He Himself bore our sins in His body on the cross, that we might die to sin and live to righteousness; for by His wounds you were healed" (1 Pet. 2:24, NASB).

The experience of salvation through Christ is definite and forever. The power and consequence of sin are real. Rescue from the power and consequence of sin takes place because God acts to bring it to pass and because man responds and permits the rescue to take place. The rescue itself has many facets that affect the individual in many ways. The next chapter deals with the many facets and implications of salvation. The purpose of this chapter is to look only at the act of rescue. We shall do so from three perspectives: (1) the nature of salvation (what it is and what it isn't); (2) the effectuation of salvation (what has to happen to bring salvation to pass); and (3) the witness to salvation (the results that testify to the reality of salvation).

THE NATURE OF SALVATION

The word *salvation* derives its meaning from the term *to save.* The word *save* means *to make whole* which comes from a root idea meaning *wholeness.* The word indicates setting free that which is bound or healing that which is wounded or broken. The concept from both the Old Testament and the New Testament most often means that a person is released from bondage. It also can mean deliverance from any kind of danger or peril. From our viewpoint, salvation is from an old existence of sin and its guilt to a new life.

Being pardoned, justified, and freed from sin and its consequences is a changing experience that brings about a radical difference in a person. One part of that difference is immediate and final. One part of that difference is as immediate as it is radical. It is the immediate movement from death into life and from condemnation to justification. There is another aspect in salvation—one that is not immediate but is continuous. This aspect is God's working in the believer to develop a new character and to nourish a new relationship between the believer and himself.

What Salvation Is Not—the Negative

Simply stated, salvation is not the result of any human effort or achievement. It is not by observing right rituals or ordinances. Belonging to a denomination is insufficient. The good we do can never be enough: "If it is by grace, it is no longer on the basis of works, otherwise grace is no longer grace" (Rom. 11:6, NASB).

Salvation cannot be obtained by education, by human struggle, through culture, or by any earthly human capability. To have gained salvation through works indicates that a person can come to a point at which he deserves to be saved. This would pervert the gospel and would render useless the death of Christ. The key in a person's relation to salvation is not that he achieves but that he receives. Salvation is God's free gift in response to faith: "The wages of sin is death, but the free gift of God is eternal life in Christ Jesus our Lord" (Rom. 6:23, NASB).

There is good reason why a person must accept salvation as a gift. It is impossible for a person to overcome the influence of evil in his life. Even if it were possible to do so, there still would be the problem of past sins and their effect. Salvation is not and will never be the result of human effort. The power of sin far surpasses any person's will to do good. Therefore, any person's attempt to become righteous and to remain righteous is doomed to failure.

By their own power and will, persons can never extricate themselves from the grip of sin. The tentacles are too strong; the shackles are welded too tightly. Rescue is possible only through what God has done in Christ.

What Salvation Is—the Positive

What, then, is the nature of salvation? It is a gift. God offers it; man receives it. The offering of the gift grows out of God's grace expressed to humanity. He desires to do far more for us than we deserve. It could be said that grace is doing for us the opposite of what we deserve. Although humanity deserves punishment and condemnation, God offers love and forgiveness.

Salvation is based on God's initiative, not man's. God initiates contact with the person, and then the person responds. "You have been born again not of seed which is perishable but imperishable, that is, through the living and abiding word of God" (1 Pet. 1:23, NASB). Gospel truth is illuminated in the mind and in the heart of a person by the Holy Spirit. Then that person yields to the truth and is born into God's family by his miraculous working operation.

PERSONAL LEARNING ACTIVITY 17
Write an answer to the following question: What does salvation in Christ mean to you? Try to give an answer that would be clear to a person who is not a Christian.

THE TRANSACTION OF SALVATION

The preceding parts of this chapter have pointed out that salvation is a gift, God is the giver, and man is the recipient. What are the elements in this transaction? What has to take place for this giving and receiving to occur?

The initiative rests with God. With convicting power, he confronts the lost person with the truth of the gospel. He makes the way of forgiveness known and offers the gift of salvation.

The necessity to respond rests with man. This response involves repentance (his attitude toward his sin) and faith (his attitude toward God). Let us examine these two more closely.

Repentance

When used in connection with salvation, repentance refers to a person's attitude toward his sin. Specifically, it refers to the fact that the person's sins have become repugnant to him and that he now acknowledges their reality with deep regret and sorrow.

Repentance is far more than a change of mind or a fear of sin's consequences. Repentance imprints on the heart a permanent attitude toward sin. The person renounces sin as Christ renounced it, hates it as Christ hated it. He repudiates it and abhors it as Christ repudiated and abhorred it. In repentance, the believer adopts God's attitude toward sin.

The Bible makes it plain that repentance is not an optional part of the salvation transaction. Rather, it is essential. "The Lord is not slow about His promise, as some count slowness, but is patient toward you, not wishing for any to perish but for all to come to repentance" (2 Pet. 3:9, NASB).

PERSONAL LEARNING ACTIVITY 18
Look up and study the meaning of the word *repentance*. Use a Bible dictionary if possible. Then study Psalm 51. Note the indications of David's repentance. Conclude the exercise by writing an honest description of your attitude toward sin.

Faith
Faith has three elements: intellectual, emotional, and volitional. Faith is an intelligent act, an act that is grounded in facts that are believed to be true. Faith is not at all the blind leap in the dark that some have declared it to be. Saving faith is grounded in the fact of the gospel and in the fact that the believer accepts those facts to be true. Faith is an intelligent act because the believer also has the testimony of other believers and the historical record of the works of God. All of these are factors that make the use of the intellect a part of the exercise of faith.

Faith is also emotional. This is not to say that the display of strong emotions is a necessary part of the faith act. Occasionally, the faith act is accompanied by the display of strong emotions. These are perfectly acceptable when they are genuine, but they are not a necessary part of exercising faith. To say that emotion is involved in faith is to say the sensibilities have been awakened to the truth of one's condition and to the truth of the gospel. In the exercise of faith, the affections of the believer are turned to Christ.

Faith is volitional, an act of the will. Saving faith is far more than feelings. It is far more than knowing and believing a body of information. Saving faith is acting on what is known and felt. Recall the earlier statement that faith is the soul leaping forth to embrace the Christ in whom it believes. Faith is complete when the person has committed himself to what he believes. The commitment involved in faith is so powerful that the truth believed lays hold of and influences the thoughts, the feelings, and the actions of the believer.

THE WITNESS TO SALVATION

Behavior and feelings vary greatly from person to person. However, a thread of consistency weaves its way through the great variety of human responses to the salvation experiences. There are some feelings and reactions that are consistent with all persons when they are saved. These uniformly consistent experiences give witness to the fact that the salvation experience has indeed taken place. These three witnesses are the internal witness, the fraternal witness, and the external witness.

The Internal Witness

When the salvation experience has taken place, the person in Christ is able to look back at the enmity that once separated him from God. He realizes with joy that he is reconciled to God; the separation no longer exists. Feeling the peace of living in God's grace is one of the internal witnesses to the fact that salvation has taken place.

Another internal witness is the sense of freedom that the Spirit gives the believer. No longer is there the sense of futility in struggling for a goal that cannot be achieved. No longer is there the self-defeating struggle to stop doing wrong and start doing right. In the salvation experience, the Savior frees man from the necessity to struggle for that which he can never attain—righteousness. He frees man from the necessity to flee from that which he can never escape—eternal death. This is the freedom that Paul referred to when he said, "There is therefore now no condemnation for those who are in Christ Jesus. For the law of the Spirit of life in Christ Jesus has set you free from the law of sin and of death" (Rom. 8:1-2, NASB).

There is a second side to the freedom that the believer receives. He is not only free from the demands of a standard he can never meet; he is free to become all that he can become in the power of the Holy Spirit.

The Fraternal Witness

The fraternal witness is fellowship grounded in God's reconciling love. Christ reconciles persons to God, persons to one another, and persons to themselves. God's people are redeemed and reconciled. The act of sharing the same redeeming, reconciling love gives believers a common unity and a unique relationship.

Sharing the joy of new life in Christ and feeling a part of the lives of other believers is possible only to those whose lives are indwelt by the Holy Spirit. Experiencing fellowship with and being at one with other believers is itself testimony to the fact that the salvation experience has taken place.

The External Witness

The life of a believer is a witness to the fact that the salvation experience has taken place. A part of the indwelling Spirit's work is to lead the believer to pattern his life after Christ's example. God is the one who enables the believer to live the Christ life. The Holy Spirit points to Christ's example and gives the believer the sources necessary to follow that example. The Christlike life is witness to the fact that the person has experienced salvation.

PERSONAL LEARNING ACTIVITY 19

Divide a sheet of paper into three columns. Label them: *internal witness, fraternal witness,* and *external witness.* List in each column the witness you experience in your own life to the fact that you are a Christian.

SUMMARY

The word *salvation* has a two-fold idea: to set free that which is bound and to heal that which is wounded. Salvation in Christ has both of these effects in the life of the believer. The salvation event takes place when the lost person trusts Christ for forgiveness. Salvation is not the result of any human attainment or achievement. It is offered by God to any who will receive it.

When a person becomes a Christian, there are three ways he can be assured of the reality of salvation. First, the Holy Spirit works in the heart of the believer and gives a sense of being at peace with God and of being free. The believer experiences a new relationship and oneness with other believers because of the common experience they share in God's reconciling love. The believer has both the desire and the power to pattern his life after Christ's life.

J. BRUCE BAUMAN/IMAGE

Salvation changes every aspect of personhood: life-style, relationships, motivations, values, and even the nature of one's existence.

Chapter 6

Salvation: the Transforming Event

[1]**trans·form**\ *tran(t)s'fȯ(ə)rm* \ vb [*ME* transformen, *fr. L* transformare, *fr.* trans- + formare *to form, fr.* forma *form*] vt **1 a:** *to change in composition or structure* **b:** *to change the outward form or appearance of* **c:** *to change in character or condition*

The salvation experience is an experience that is filled with wonder and the unexpected. No matter how clearly the salvation experience has been described and explained, there is no way the individual can be prepared for what actually happens. No other experience in life brings about so radical a change. The chapter title declares salvation to be a transforming event. This is an accurate description, because every aspect of a person's being is touched and is transformed. "Therefore if any man is in Christ, he is a new creature; the old things passed away; behold, new things have come" (2 Cor. 5:17, NASB).

The changes produced by salvation are so numerous, so radical, and so far-reaching that no single word or phrase can describe them all fully. Baptists and other Christian groups use a number of words and phrases to list, to differentiate, and to define the many changes that are a part of the salvation experience.

PERSONAL LEARNING ACTIVITY 20
Before studying further, write your own definitions of the following terms: *regeneration, conversion, sanctification, perseverance, adoption, reconciliation,* and *justification.*

As you study this chapter, you will study the terms in the preceding personal learning activity. You will see how every aspect of personhood is changed: life-style, relationships, motivations, values, and even the nature of one's existence. You will see how some of these changes are immediate while others are not complete after a lifetime.

Also, as you study this chapter, you should bear in mind an important principle. The salvation event is a singular event. It is an event with numerous aspects that affect the individual in a number of different ways. Salvation in some respects is immediate and final. For example, being raised from spiritual death to spiritual life is immediate, irrevocable, and final. Other aspects of salvation such as forgiveness are repeated over and over in the life of the saved person. A third perspective on salvation is that it is a process that begins at the time of conversion and continues throughout the life of the believer. Sanctification is an example of this aspect of salvation.

As you study this chapter, you will study several different terms that describe different aspects of the salvation event. Remember that salvation does not happen in installments. It is a singular event. The terms studied in this chapter all examine the same event but from different perspectives.

REGENERATION: THE NEW BIRTH

John 3
Now there was a man of the Pharisees, named Nicodemus, a ruler of the Jews;

2 this man came to Him by night, and said to Him, "Rabbi, we know that You have come from God as a teacher; for no one can do these signs that You do unless God is with him."

3 Jesus answered and said unto him, "Truly, truly, I say to you, unless one is born again, he cannot see the kingdom of God."

4 Nicodemus said to Him, "How can a man be born when he is old? He cannot enter a second time into his mother's womb and be born, can he?"

> 5 Jesus answered, "Truly, truly, I say to you, unless one is born of water and the Spirit, he cannot enter into the kingdom of God.
> 6 "That which is born of the flesh is flesh; and that which is born of the Spirit is spirit.
> 7 "Do not marvel that I said to you, 'You must be born again.' "
>
> NASB

Jesus spoke to Nicodemus about the necessity of being born again. He was speaking of the same experience that we also describe as the new birth and as regeneration. Being brought out of spiritual death into spiritual life cannot express all the ideas that are a part of the salvation experience. However, this term does so more nearly than any of the other terms do. The term *regeneration* speaks specifically of being brought from spiritual death into spiritual life. However, all the other concepts studied in this chapter are at least implied in the idea of having been dead and now being alive.

Regeneration refers to a change in one's moral and spiritual nature. This change is necessary because of one's nature as a sinner. Recall that chapter 1 pointed out that the real problem of sin is at the center of a person's being. Sin has tainted and has distorted the image of God within us. Inwardly, our hearts do not conform to God's holiness. The part of a person that can be seen—his life—is generally a manifestation of what he is within. His actions serve as a mirror to reflect his motives, values, and goals.

By force of will and self-discipline a person may be able to change his actions. But it is impossible to bring about a change in one's moral and spiritual nature. The power for such a transformation must come from a source outside the individual. The transformation must be effected by someone other than the one being transformed. Regeneration is wrought by God's divine power as the Holy Spirit transforms the believer's inner person. A new moral and spiritual nature is imparted. The marred image of God is recreated.

PERSONAL LEARNING ACTIVITY 21
Read Ephesians 2:1-10. Then identify the words or phrases that relate to the following facts about regeneration:
1. **Man's inner condition as a sinner is the cause of spiritual death.**
2. **A person's actions are indications of the fact that he is spiritually dead.**
3. **Regeneration is a divine work.**
4. **A person's actions are indications of the fact that he has been born again.**

CONVERSION: A NEW ORIENTATION

> Acts 3
> 26 "For you first, God raised up His Servant, and sent Him to bless you by turning every one of you from your wicked ways."
> NASB

Conversion is turning away from sin toward God. The two elements are essential to each other and cannot be separated. When one genuinely turns away from sin, there is but one direction to turn: toward God. The converse is also true. One cannot turn toward God unless he has first turned away from sin. This is the deliberate act of will by which the individual turns his life from the direction in which it is traveling and redirects it toward God.

Conversion naturally speaks of a transformation in the way a person lives. But the real significance in conversion is the transformation of the values and motives that determine how the life is lived. Conversion is also the deliberate act of will by which a person turns his values and motives toward God. Conversion, therefore, is more than a reversal in the direction of one's life. It is a reversal in the perspective out of which life is lived. It is more than a renunciation of sin. It is a renunciation of the inner condition that leads to sin.

Two important facts about conversion should be observed. First, conversion is closely related to repentance and faith. It is impossible to speak of a transformation in values, motives, and life direction without repentance and faith coming into play. One cannot turn away from sin unless repentance is a reality. Neither can one turn toward God unless he exercises faith to do so.

The second important fact to be observed is that conversion is possible because of God's initiative. Man has no power of will by which he can turn from sin to God. He has not the resources with which to transform the perspective out of which he lives his life. The Holy Spirit makes available to man the power to turn. If a person does turn away from sin toward God, it is because he has accepted the Spirit's enabling power to do so.

Zaccheus' conversion began with a deep realization of his need. One day he saw Jesus Christ coming in the crowd. The stories of Christ's teachings and works were so significant to him that he wanted to see this prophet in person. After Christ called Zaccheus to come from the tree, an encounter took place that transformed Zaccheus' character, behavior, and principles of action. The Scriptures take note of the intense change in his total thinking, life, and relationships (Luke 19:1-10).

Nicodemus was a great intellectual, noted as a significant ruler among the Jews; his religious stature was well respected. Nicodemus came to Jesus to find truth. His insatiable desire to know more of the truth gripped his spirit and sent him in search of truth even in spite of great personal risk.

Jesus cut across all extraneous matters and spoke to his real need. The conversion was enough to change Nicodemus' entire makeup. The dialogue that started intellectually soon reshaped his concept of God, of himself, and of the meaning of life. Although the Scriptures do not record Nicodemus' conversion, both history and tradition attest to it. History records that after Jesus died on the cross, Nicodemus went with Joseph of Arimathea to bury him in a manner befitting a person of the Jewish heritage. Other occasions gave indication he truly turned from the old way and spoke his new life-experience.

Saul of Tarsus had a religious fervor that drove him to search out and to destroy the Christians. One day on the road to Damascus Saul was confronted by Jesus Christ. The background to this event probably began early when he learned of Christ's teachings. He certainly saw the evidence of what Christ had done in the life of deacon Stephen.

Now on the road to Damascus Paul had a turnaround. He halted in his way of life. Christ changed not only his name but his life. Paul's new experience moved him to set his face in new directions. Much of the New Testament comes to us from the pen of this great apostle to the Gentiles. He served Christ well and bore the marks of his changed life.

Conversion is turning from sin to serve the living and true God. The heart is turned from evil to good, from darkness to light, from the power of Satan to God. One is turned from frustration to victory, from being a slave to sin to being a conqueror of sin. Conversion involves the exchange of slavery for servanthood. Once a slave to sin, now one becomes a servant of God.

FORGIVENESS AND JUSTIFICATION: A NEW STANDING

> Acts 13
>
> 38 "Therefore let it be known to you, brethren, that through Him forgiveness of sins is proclaimed to you,
>
> 39 "and through Him everyone who believes is freed from all things, from which you could not be freed through the Law of Moses."
>
> Romans 5
>
> 16 The gift is not like that which came through the one who sinned; for on the one hand the judgment arose from one transgression resulting in the condemnation, but on the other hand the free gift arose from many transgressions resulting in justification.
>
> 17 For if by the transgression of the one, death reigned through the one, much more those who receive the abundance of grace and of the gift of righteousness will reign in life through the One, Jesus Christ.
>
> 18 So then as through one transgression there resulted condemnation to all men, even so through one act of righteousness there resulted justification of life to all men.
>
> NASB

Forgiveness and justification are opposite sides of the same coin. They both describe what God does about the sin that keeps man from standing with him in a personal relationship. Sin affects one's relationship with God in two ways. Sin is both an affront to God's nature and a violation of his law. Therefore, there are both interpersonal and legal implications in what God does to transform the sinner's standing before him.

Forgiveness

Forgiveness is the "sending away" of sin. The individual is released from the guilt of sin. Remission of the punishment against sin which is eternal death is both real and necessary: " 'Therefore let it be known to you, brethren, that through Him forgiveness of sins is proclaimed to you' " (Acts 13:38, NASB); "There is therefore now no condemnation for those who are in Christ Jesus" (Rom. 8:1, NASB).

Forgiveness of sin absolves guilt and, therefore, does away with the necessity for punishment. Because we are human, we may find it difficult to understand how a holy God can forgive sin. We find it extremely difficult to forgive; but God forgives gladly. Divine love makes the difference.

Justification

Justification is the judicial act of God by which he declares the sinner to be free from condemnation and restores him to divine favor. By his sin, man has violated God's divine law. As a violator of God's law, the sinner is guilty and is condemned because of that guilt. But when the sinner responds to God in faith, God replaces the charge of guilt and condemnation with acquittal and acceptance.

The concept of justification also contains the idea of being made righteous. In fact, the same Greek noun is translated in our English Scriptures as both *righteousness* and *justification*. The same Greek verb is translated as both *declare righteous* and *justify*. Justification is far more than a legal term. When God justifies the sinner, the character and nature of God's personhood come into play. The result of forgiveness and of justification is that the sinner stands in a personal relationship with God. This personal relationship is possible because God regards the believer as a righteous person (2 Cor. 5:21).

To be regarded by God as being righteous does not mean that

the person is indeed righteous. It means that the person is set forth as righteous in a legal sense: "For if Abraham was justified by works, he has something to boast about; but not before God. For what does the Scripture say? 'And Abraham believed God, and it was reckoned to him as righteousness.' Now to the one who works, his wage is not reckoned as a favor but as what is due. But to the one who does not work, but believes in Him who justified the ungodly, his faith is reckoned as righteousness, just as David also speaks of the blessing upon the man to whom God reckons righteousness apart from works: 'Blessed are those whose lawless deeds have been forgiven, and whose sins have been covered. Blessed is the man whose sin the Lord will not take into account' " (Rom. 4:2-8, NASB).

Justification is based on Christ's redemptive work. When a sinner trusts Christ, he is accepted by God because of his faith instead of being condemned because of his sin.

RECONCILIATION: A NEW RELATIONSHIP

> Colossians 1
> 19 For it was the Father's good pleasure for all the fulness to dwell in Him,
> 20 and through Him to reconcile all things to Himself, having made peace through the blood of His cross; through Him, I say, whether things on earth or things in heaven.
> 21 And although you were formerly alienated and hostile in mind, engaged in evil deeds,
> 22 yet He has now reconciled you in His fleshly body through death, in order to present you before Him holy and blameless and beyond reproach—
>
> NASB

Reconciliation is the restoring of a relationship between two persons. The fact that the Scriptures speak of a reconciliation between God and man assumes that man is alienated from God. By his sin, the sinner separates himself from God. The nature of the broken relationship is not one of God's not being on speaking terms with us because he is hurt or angry. Rather, the presence of sin in a person's life makes impossible the relationship that Christ has already died to make possible.

There is no relationship—not because God wants it that way, but because sin forces it to be that way. Reconciliation is the restoration of the relationship that sin had destroyed. Obviously, sin must be removed for reconciliation to be a possibility. It is at this point that the sinner is helpless to effect reconciliation. It is God who removes the guilt of sin. Therefore, reconciliation is God's work. It is Christ who reconciles man and God.

Reconciliation should not be understood as an act directed to God to appease his anger. The opposite is true. Reconciliation is God's act of love to bring back and to restore to fellowship and to relationship those who have estranged themselves from him.

ADOPTION: A NEW FAMILY

> Romans 8
> 15 For you have not received a spirit of slavery leading to fear again, but you have received a spirit of adoption as sons by which we cry out, "Abba! Father!"
> 16 The Spirit Himself bears witness with our spirit that we are children of God,
> 17 and if children, heirs also, heirs of God and fellow-heirs with Christ, if indeed we suffer with Him in order that we may also be glorified with Him.
>
> NASB

Adoption is the admission of an outsider to some or all the privileges of a natural child. When the term is used in relation to the salvation experience, it refers to the fact that believers become God's children. It also points out the fact that although we are God's by creation, sin has destroyed that relationship. Therefore, adoption is necessary to restore to us the rights we forfeited by our sin.

Paul referred to the concept of adoption and to the fact that we are God's children. And he spoke of the blessings that result from the father/child relationship. All persons are created to be God's children, and God's will is that it be so. However, only those who have experienced the new birth become children of God.

The term *adoption* also has legal connotations. It is saying that in the face of the law that once condemned us, God not only justifies us but also takes us to himself to be his children. Where the law once built a barrier between us and God, God now makes us legal heirs with all the rights of the household. Faith is the doorway to sonship. It is through faith that one receives all the rights of the household. This is a new relationship and a new life with which the past has nothing to do. "As many as received Him, to them He gave the right to become children of God, even to those who believe in His name" (John 1:12, NASB).

The Scriptures speak clearly about the results of becoming a child and an heir of the heavenly Father. First, we have the presence of the Holy Spirit in our lives assuring us that we are the children of God. "In order that He might redeem those who were under the Law, that we might receive the adoption as sons. And because you are sons, God has sent forth the Spirit of His Son into our hearts, crying, 'Abba! Father!' " (Gal. 4:5-6, NASB). A place in the Father's house is promised: "Jesus answered and said to him, 'If anyone loves Me, he will keep My word; and My Father will love him, and We will come to him, and make Our abode with him' " (John 14:23, NASB). God's eternal kingdom is given for inheritance: " 'Then the King will say to those on His right, "Come, you who are blessed of My Father, inherit the kingdom prepared for you from the foundation of the world" ' " (Matt. 25:34, NASB). Salvation provides the right to be heirs of God and joint heirs with Christ (Rom. 8).

The adopted person loses all rights to the old family to gain more and better rights in the new family. The old life has no more rights over a person. God has absolute rights. God's children receive a nature that trusts him, obeys him, and becomes increasingly intimate with him. The change in the believer's nature and his adoption assures him the full blessings of God's kingdom. As an adopted child, the Christian is bound legally and eternally to the Father. In a miracle of divine love and mercy, God takes lost, helpless, debt-burdened, poverty-stricken sinners, births them into his family through regeneration, and adopts them legally through Christ. In one action, the debts are canceled; the alienation is ended; glory is inherited.

SANCTIFICATION: A NEW LIFE-STYLE

> Romans 12
> I urge you therefore, brethren, by the mercies of God, to present your bodies a living and holy sacrifice, acceptable to God, which is your spiritual service of worship.
> 2 And do not be conformed to this world, but be transformed by the renewing of your mind, that you may prove what the will of God is, that which is good and acceptable and perfect.
> NASB

Sanctification means being separated from that which is ungodlike and being set apart to God for God's purpose. In its New Testament sense, the term refers specifically to two aspects of the salvation experience. First, the term is used to refer to the result of redemption. Saved persons are referred to as saints or as the sanctified ones. The implication is that God once and for all has brought us apart from the dominion of sin and has set us apart for himself. The term is positional in that it refers to man's relationship with God.

There is also a second aspect to the concept of sanctification. Sanctification is also experiential—a continuing experience in the life of the believer. This aspect of the term refers to the process by which the believer wins day by day the victory over the influence of sin in his life. This is the gradual, painful elimination of the strongholds and pockets of sin in the life. Experiential sanctification is the process of growing in the likeness of Christ, of becoming more like the Father, and of being more able to know and to do his will.

PERSEVERANCE: A NEW ASSURANCE

> Romans 5
> 8 But God demonstrates His own love toward us, in that while we were yet sinners, Christ died for us.

> 9 Much more then, having now been justified by His blood, we shall be saved from the wrath of God through Him.
>
> 10 For if while we were enemies, we were reconciled to God through the death of His Son, much more, having been reconciled, we shall be saved by His life.
>
> NASB

Perseverance refers to the fact that God enables his children to continue steadfastly in faith and in obedience. The knowledge of God's enabling power in one's life gives the Christian a new assurance for living. The lost person experiences nothing but frustration, hopelessness, and defeat in trying to understand and to cope with life. The work of the Holy Spirit is to transform that attitude to one of radiant confidence and anticipation. This confidence and anticipation are made possible by the Christian's knowledge that he will endure.

The fact of the new birth is assured by God's covenant; and his people must be understood to be his purchased possession. "You are a chosen race, a royal priesthood, a holy nation, a people for God's own possession, that you may proclaim the excellencies of Him who has called you out of the darkness into His marvelous light" (1 Pet. 2:9, NASB). The believer is kept by the power of God through faith. A person does not keep himself; God does the keeping. "Who are protected by the power of God through faith for a salvation ready to be revealed in the last time" (1 Pet. 1:5, NASB).

Paul said that no thing or item of human experience can separate from the love of God: "Who shall separate us from the love of Christ? Shall tribulation, or distress, or persecution, or famine, or nakedness, or peril. or sword? Just as it is written, 'For Thy sake we are being put to death all day long; we were considered as sheep to be slaughtered.' But in all these things we overwhelmingly conquer through Him who loved us. For I am convinced that neither death, nor life, nor angels, nor principalities, nor things present, nor things to come, nor powers, nor height, nor depth, nor any other created thing, shall be able to separate us from the love of God, which is in Christ Jesus our Lord" (Rom. 8:35-39, NASB). He was convinced that nothing could destroy this relationship. Even Satan cannot destroy the relationship so long as a person is connected to God's love by faith.

We can rest our assurance of final salvation upon God's love. "Hope does not disappoint, because the love of God has been poured out within our hearts through the Holy Spirit who was given to us. But God demonstrates His own love toward us, in that while we were yet sinners, Christ died for us" (Rom. 5:5,8, NASB). We believe in the steadfast love of God; it is a love that will not let us go. Ultimate victory is assured. The unequivocal declaration of Christ is that the believer shall never perish: " 'I give eternal life to them, and they shall never perish; and no one shall snatch them out of My hand. My Father, who has given them to Me, is greater than all; and no one is able to snatch them out of the Father's hand' " (John 10:28-29, NASB).

Believing in Christ gives assurance of eternal life and dispels spiritual condemnation: " 'Truly, truly, I say to you, he who hears My Word, and believes Him who sent Me, has eternal life, and does not come into judgment, but has passed out of death into life' " (John 5:24, NASB). Salvation's assurance is very clear: "And whom He predestined, these He also called; and whom He called, these He also justified; and whom He justified, these He also glorified" (Rom. 8:30, NASB).

God works to accomplish his purpose in the life of the believer. And God does not fail. The believer's existence is not a self-contained or a self-sustained life. It is life sustained by the grace of the same Savior and Lord through whom one is justified.

God wills to preserve the believers. The newborn person will persevere because it is God's will for him to do so. Perseverance is not dependent on the believer's will or strength. Rather, it is based on God's ability to keep the promise he has to keep his children safe.

PERSONAL LEARNING ACTIVITY 22
Review the definitions that you wrote in Personal Learning Activity 20. Make any desired additions or changes in your definitions. Then write your own summary for this chapter.

SUMMARY

FOR FURTHER STUDY

Stagg, Frank. *New Testament Theology.* Nashville: Broadman Press, 1962, chapter 4.

Hobbs, Herschel H. *The Baptist Faith and Message.* Nashville: Convention Press, 1971.

Those who gather in Christ's name embody the life of Christ and exemplify that life to one another and to all people.

Chapter 7

Salvation: a New Way of Life

As wonderful as heaven must be, God's initial purpose in salvation is not to have us there with him—else he would transport us there immediately upon our conversion. There must be something more important to God than having us in heaven with him. And the thing that is of primary importance to God must have something to do with this world since he leaves us in it after conversion.

When I came to know Christ as my Savior, no one told me of the continuing joy I could experience in the Christian life. Nor did any person help me understand the responsibilities that are a part of the new life. A year passed before I became a member of a local congregation of believers and began my pilgrimage of faith. Since then, my life has been one of a journey into maturity. I have discovered Christianity to be more than a philosophy or a creed. It is a way of life. Out of my own experience, I would like to share with you at least three settings in which the Christian life expresses itself: in the church, in the family, and in the community.

THE CHURCH

In the minds of most Baptists the term *church* has two meanings. It can be understood to refer to the institution or to the people. Sometimes the term is used without attempting to draw a distinction between the shades of meaning. The term is used in this chapter to refer to God's people. Even in those paragraphs that refer to the church working or to the church meeting, the emphasis is not upon the institution but upon the gathered people. When the term is used in the New Testament, it is used most often to refer to a local assembly of Christian believers. They are the people of God called out to be distinct from the world.

The church is more than one of the settings in which the Christian life expresses itself. A relationship with the church is essential to the Christian life. To Christ, the gathering of believers was not an incidental part of their relationship with him; it was an essential one. He said to Peter, "Upon this rock I will build my church." The church is described as a body made up of fellowshipping believers, and the life of that body is dependent upon its living relationship with Christ (Eph. 4:11-16).

The church is God's new creation, a redeemed people in the midst of an estranged humanity. The life of this redeemed fellowship, the body of Christ, manifests Christ to the world. As the church, this newborn community becomes the lighthouse, even the light of the world. They offer hope to those who need hope and strength to those who are weak. This redeemed order in the midst of the world is the voice of God calling clearly to the joy of salvation. Moreover, the church speaks authoritatively against social evils and proclaims truth where truth needs to be proclaimed. It is the people of God who declare the good news that salvation is to be found in none other than Jesus Christ. Christ's followers are the instrument by which the gospel is shared with unbelievers. One of the easiest and most natural settings in which the Christian life can express itself is the fellowship of other believers.

As a redeemed community, different persons of all backgrounds and ages join in one thought and unite in one truth. Wherever there are Christians, there is the church. They have a wide range of experiences, thoughts, and views in common and meet each other in the context of similar feelings, needs, and purposes.

The believer's new life in Christ embodies all that Christ stands for. Those who gather in Christ's name embody the life of Christ and exemplify that life to one another and to all people. The church is essential to the Christian life. It is in the context of the church that the believer is able to receive the support, the encouragement, and the spiritual nourishment that Christ intends for every believer. The church provides the context for at least three occurrences of the Christian life: baptism, fellowship, and growth in responsible Christian living.

Baptism

Baptism should be one of the first occurrences in the life of a new believer. This event relates the believer to his new life in Christ. It is a picture of salvation that shows that one has passed from an old life of sin, through death to be raised to a new life with Christ. "What shall we say then? Are we to continue in sin that grace might increase? May it never be! How shall we who died to sin still live in it? Or do you not know that all of us who have been baptized into Christ Jesus have been baptized into His death? Therefore we have been buried with Him through baptism into death, in order that as Christ was raised from the dead through the glory of the Father, so we too might walk in newness of life. For if we have become united with Him in the likeness of His death, certainly we shall be also in the likeness of His resurrection, knowing this, that our old self was crucified with Him, that our body of sin might be done away with, that we should no longer be slaves to sin" (Rom. 6:1-6, NASB).

Baptism Identifies the New Believer with Christ

The joy of being saved makes a Christian want to be identified with Christ. Being identified publicly with Christ by baptism is giving testimony that one has abandoned the old way of life for a new way of life, that the new birth is real, and that one's life is made new. Baptism is a public statement of one's intent to live for Christ through love, through devotion, and by obedience to his will.

Baptism Identifies the New Believer with God's People

Sharing the experience of baptism with other Christians identifies the new believer with God's children who form his church. This identification expresses a united faith, a common cause, a common belief, and a common relationship. The relationship with other believers is one of the greatest joys of the Christian life. Almost without exception, identification with other believers is a natural result of the salvation experience. This identification grows out of a deep bond of fellowship, shared concern, and mutual responsibility between believers. Since baptism is a requirement for membership in local Baptist congregations, the act itself becomes an indication of one's identification with the believers who make up the local congregation.

Baptism Identifies the New Believer with Christ's Mission
Christ's purpose is to bring all people into a reconciling relationship with the Father. Paul said, "He made Him who knew no sin to be sin on our behalf, that we might become the righteousness of God in Him" (2 Cor. 5:21, NASB). The new life in Christ is dynamic and exciting. In the new life, the believer is identified with Christ and his people, and with Christ's mission for his people. Being identified with Christ's mission is the result of coming to grips with one's personal responsibility to let others know that Christ is the only hope of rescue from sin.

Christ is the head of the body, the church: "He put all things in subjection under His feet, and gave Him as head over all things to the church" (Eph. 1:22, NASB). The function of the body is to respond to his instructions. It is illogical to think that a person can become a part of Christ and not be responsive to his leadership and a participant in Christ's ongoing purpose of redemption.

Fellowship
A second reason why the church is essential to the Christian life is that the church provides the context for fellowship. The church is a group of believers who are bound to God and to one another through the experience of saving grace in Christ. They are welded into unity by the Holy Spirit. They worship God and grow in fellowship with one another.

The new birth makes possible a new relationship with God. This new relationship generates fellowship with others who have had a similar experience. This group of believers are banded together in the unity of oneness through Christ. Their distinct identity with Christ, with Christ's mission, and with one another has been marked by their baptism. Their lives embody the expression of redemption. One of the marks of God's people is that the Holy Spirit has transformed them into a living, loving, spiritual fellowship.

Another of the wonders and glories of this united company of the redeemed is its composition. They come from every conceivable cultural, economic, and educational background. They all share the same Christ and the same salvation. They have the privilege of sharing the same worship, the same joy, and the same fellowship. The people of the church are not perfect. They are ordinary people—weak and human. The common denominator in their fellowship is each individual's relationship with Christ.

Although there are weaknesses, human failures, and imperfections, these people are welded together by the Holy Spirit. There is something more than the gathering of persons when they are in one place. When Christians gather to worship, it is their fellowship with Christ that draws them together. Worship is at the heart of what believers share. It is also the mainspring of much the church is to do. Worship is a recognition of God's worth and a response to God's revelation of himself to us in Christ.

This fellowship that believers have together makes it possible for them to share all life's experiences: their common struggles, prayers, sufferings, losses, even victories. They share with one another because, in the Holy Spirit, each person is a part of every other person. The church is the family of God. They are his new people, brought into being by the death and resurrection of Jesus and indwelt by the Holy Spirit.

The new birth begins a new life for the believer. Learning to live the Christian life and developing one's ability to overcome in the daily inner struggle with self and with sin is a difficult and trying task. The new believer needs a caring, supportive environment in which to live out his commitment to Christ. The fellowship of God's children, the church, provides such an environment.

Responsible Christian Living

A third reason the church is important to the new believer is that the church provides the context for growth in responsible Christian living. One distinguishing mark of the church is that believers feel they should live responsibly in relationship with other believers and in relationship with the community. Responsible, Christlike living is a continuing public confession that Jesus is the Savior and the Lord.

It was at Antioch that Christ's followers were first called Christians. They were given this name because their following Christ as Lord had made an observable difference in their lives. The regenerate life should be characterized by Christlikeness. Every believer's life should reflect the truth that Paul stated about his own life: " 'I have been crucified with Christ; and it is no longer I who live, but Christ lives in me; and the life which I now live in the flesh I live by faith in the Son of God, who loved me, and delivered Himself up for me' " (Gal. 2:20, NASB).

The church provides the best context for learning to live a responsible Christian life. Two important elements of the responsible Christian life are spiritual growth and witnessing. The fellowship of other believers serves to facilitate both.

Spiritual Growth

The goal for every believer is that he should be like Christ. "Grow in the grace and knowledge of our Lord and Savior Jesus Christ. To Him be the glory, both now and to the day of eternity. Amen" (2 Pet. 3:18, NASB). However, this likeness does not automatically occur upon conversion; it must be grown into. Life in Christ should be characterized as one of progress and spiritual activity. The result of that progress and activity should be that the believer becomes progressively more able to emulate Christ in his own life.

This growth hardly takes place for the believer whose life is lived in isolation from all other believers. The new believer needs help in understanding the meaning of this new birth and the new life he is to live. He needs help understanding the basic teachings of the Bible. The church provides the environment of Bible study, prayer, worship, and fellowship in which spiritual growth can take place most easily.

Witnessing

A believer's desire to bring others to know Christ is a spontaneous impulse born out of a deepened concern for the lost. Witnessing is not incidental or secondary in the believer's new life. It is not only a natural desire, it is also a responsibility.

The desire to share one's experience with others is illustrated by the encounter the woman in Samaria had with Jesus. This woman of shameful character was made whole when Jesus shared with her the miracle of new life. Immediately she ran back to those among whom she had sinned to cry, " 'Come, see a man who told me all the things that I have done; this is not the Christ, is it?' " (John 4:29, NASB).

The church is important to the believer's growth in witnessing. The fellowship of other witnesses encourages the believer and counteracts the indifferent or hostile response often given by unsaved persons. Being in a fellowship of witnessing believers helps keep one aware of the degree of his own concern for the lost. It also places the believer's witness in the total context of what God is doing in the world and among his people.

PERSONAL LEARNING ACTIVITY 23
Below are several terms that refer to the church. Beside each, write one or two words that the term brings to mind. For example, you may want to write *Christlikeness* beside *Christian*.
***Bride of Christ* (Rev. 19:7-10)** ______________________
***Body of Christ* (Eph. 4:11-16)** ______________________
***Building, holy temple* (1 Cor. 3:9-16)** ______________________
***Holy nation* (1 Pet. 2:9-12)** ______________________
***Royal priesthood* (1 Pet. 2:9-12)** ______________________
***God's own people* (1 Pet. 2:9-12)** ______________________
***Christians* (Acts 11:26)** ______________________
***Family of God* (2 Cor. 6:14-18)** ______________________
Now study each passage referred to above. Are there additional ideas you can add to what you have already written?

THE FAMILY

The family is another setting in which the Christian life expresses itself. The Bible speaks plainly of the responsibility family members have to live Christlike lives in relationship with one another (Eph. 6:1-4; Col. 3:18-21). One way this relationship expresses itself is the desire on the part of one family member to bring other family members to know Christ.

The Scriptures record that Andrew went to tell Peter, his brother, " 'We have found the Messiah,' " and Philip found Nathaniel and told him, " 'We have found Him of whom Moses in the Law and also the Prophets wrote, Jesus of Nazareth' " (John 1:41,45, NASB). When the Philippian jailer was converted, one of his first concerns was for the other members of his family (Acts 16:22-34).

It is a beautiful and an impressive experience to see Christian parents accepting their God-given responsibility to train their children to love and to serve God. Family life is the happiest and most complete when family members relate to one another as Christians. The Christian life expressed within the context of the family is basic to and serves as the pattern for all the other relationships of life. The Christian life expresses itself in the family as Christian family members relate to one another in love as brothers and as sisters in Christ. The example of relationships in the Christian family serves as an ideal for all other relationships between persons.

The family where every person is not a believer is another setting in which the Christian life expresses itself. Often, it is very difficult for children to relate as Christians to parents who are not Christians, or a husband or a wife to relate to a spouse who is not a Christian. Yet, it is equally important that the Christian life be expressed lovingly and patiently in this less sympathetic family setting. It is often because of the Christian behavior of one member of a family that other family members are won eventually (1 Cor. 7:12-16). Also, the Christian behavior of one family member is sometimes the only stabilizing force in the family during times of crisis.

The family is the basic unit of society. If believers are to express their Christian faith at any point, it should be here.

PERSONAL LEARNING ACTIVITY 24

The discussion of the relationship of the family to the Christian life is brief but important. List things that in your judgment strengthen the Christian home.

1.
2.
3.
4.
5.

Make a second list of things that in your judgment weaken and work against the Christian home.

1.
2.
3.
4.
5.

Now reflect on both lists and think how the church can go about encouraging Christian homes to include the content of your first list and eliminate the content of the second list.

THE COMMUNITY

The third setting in which the Christian life expresses itself is the community. Christ taught that if his followers were serious, their lives would not only be a reflection of his style of living but they also would change the structural relationships and the fabric of living about them. Every new believer becomes a new strand in the fabric of affairs and in history. The believer's relationship to society should always be a reflection of Christ.

Positive Christian Living

Living as a Christian citizen in today's society demands that Christ be portrayed. The greatest statement of Christian conduct and character is found in the consistent Christian life. The distinctiveness of the Christian life is evident to those who are not Christians. This distinctiveness is not accidental. It is the reality of the believer's faith being manifested in his deeds.

The Christian citizen has a place in a non-Christian world. He lives as a good and responsible person. Christian citizenship strengthens law-abiding conduct, muzzles the tongue of foolish gossip, and lives the gospel in the circle of society among friends, at work, and in the community. Whatever one is and whatever one does should be a display of the character of Christ.

As a member of the community, the believer is unique because he is governed by a moral discernment that is not determined by the average level of community thinking. He is governed by the pattern of Christ and the principle of living he taught and demonstrated.

Jesus talked of how the kingdom of heaven acts as a leavening power in the world: "He spoke another parable to them, 'The kingdom of heaven is like leaven, which a woman took, and hid in three pecks of meal, until it was all leavened' " (Matt. 13:33, NASB).

Christ declared himself to be the light of the world: "Again therefore Jesus spoke to them, saying, 'I am the light of the world; he who follows Me shall not walk in the darkness, but shall have the light of life' " (John 8:12, NASB); " 'While I am in the world, I am the light of the world' " (John 9:5, NASB). The people of God in Christ are also the light of the world: " 'You are the light of the world. A city set on a hill cannot be hidden' " (Matt. 5:14, NASB). They are the salt of the earth: " 'You are the salt of the earth; but if the salt has become tasteless, how will it be made salty again? It is good for nothing any more, except to be thrown out and trampled under foot by men' " (Matt. 5:13, NASB). The Christian life expresses itself in the community as leaven, as light, and as salt. The teaching is obvious: the Christian life should express itself in the community in such a way that is makes a difference for good.

Christ taught that the perfect character of God the Father was to be the believer's goal. Characterized by a new brand of righteousness, believers should not be satisfied with the average standard. " 'For I say to you, that unless your righteousness surpasses that of the scribes and Pharisees, you shall not enter the kingdom of heaven' " (Matt. 5:20, NASB). The Christ-person has the challenge to live beyond the norm accepted by conventional religion.

Christ's salvation really makes people act right in their world rather than withdraw from it. Withdrawal neither impresses nor changes the community.

Jesus said that the fruitful Christian life would clearly identify beyond shadow of a doubt all those who are his followers. All who believe God, who receive the gospel and publicly profess their faith in Christ excel in such good works: "This is a trustworthy statement; and concerning these things I want you to speak confidently, so that those who have believed God may be careful to engage in good deeds. These things are good and profitable for men. But shun foolish controversies and genealogies and strife and disputes about the Law; for they are unprofitable and worthless. Reject a factious man after a first and second warning, knowing that such a man is perverted and is sinning, being self-condemned" (Titus 3:8-11, NASB). A person is saved *for* works. A salvation that does not produce a moral and ethical effect upon life and character leaves itself open to serious questions about its validity.

Witnessing for Today as Well as for Eternity

Witnessing the gospel to persons who are not Christians is the greatest opportunity of service and growth for the believer. Christ entrusted believers with the responsibility to continue the work he began. " 'The Son of Man has come to seek and to save that which was lost' " (Luke 19:10, NASB). The mission of witness is clearly expressed: "Jesus said to them, 'Follow Me, and I will make you become fishers of men' " (Mark 1:17, NASB). Christ's final words to his disciples leave no doubt about the content of the message and responsibility for its delivery: "Jesus therefore said to them again, 'Peace be with you; as the Father has sent Me, I also send you' " (John 20:21, NASB). "He said to them, 'Thus it is written, that the Christ should suffer and rise again from the dead the third day; and that repentance for forgiveness of sins should be proclaimed in His name to all the nations, beginning from Jerusalem. You are witnesses of these things' " (Luke 24:46-48, NASB).

Positive witness changes individuals. Changed individuals change society. This is the hope for humanity. The ideal for society is for changed individuals to become society changers. God wishes to influence the total area of human life. Therefore, the believer should not acquiesce to the society. Rather, he should be a catalyst for good. Salvation sends the saved ones into the world to Christianize it and to develop and maintain new standards.

Salvation is not to be identified with any social, economic, or political movement, or any human organization. God's kingdom transcends but should also transform all human relations, activities, and movements. Changing persons change social conditions. It is wrong to think our first task is to change society and that better conditions will make persons better. History has disclosed the error of such thinking. The way to change life and living circumstances is to change the persons who make up the structures of life.

The grace of God does make life better and conditions more livable. Examine societies where Christians have had a direct influence. One would be a poor Christian who does not see the value of working to counter the effect of evil in the community. The beginning point in changing social conditions is to share the reality of salvation in Christ with those who do not know him. The more who come to Christ in salvation, the more attitudes and personal actions are changed and the more different the community will be.

The Christian must bear in mind also that active witnessing is only the beginning point in responsible citizenship. Jesus was concerned about the whole person. He fed people and healed people; he condemned exploiters and predators and any raw uses of power. Christian citizenship must combine witnessing and working to change social structures and to correct social injustices. To do anything else is to divide the gospel.

PERSONAL LEARNING ACTIVITY 25

The final section of this chapter deals with the Christian's social responsibilities. There follows a list of critical social issues. Please look at them carefully and then give them a priority number from one to ten.

__Street crime
__Poverty
__Abortion
__Pollution
__Corruption in government
__Housing
__Pornography
__Divorce
__Energy
__Racial and ethnic concerns

Decide whether the church should take a stand on these issues and how Christians can let their influence be felt on these issues.

SUMMARY

The new life in Christ must express itself as surely as our physical bodies must breathe. To refuse or to stifle this expression is to smother the very life out of the believer's newfound joy. There are three settings in which the Christian life expresses itself: the church, the home, and the community.

The Christian life should express itself in the fellowship of other believers because of the need for instruction, support, and encouragement. It is in the loving, caring fellowship of other Christians that the believer is best able to grow to be more like Christ and to learn to live responsibly as a child of God.

The home is the basic unit of our society. If the Christian faith is to be expressed at any point in today's world, it should be in the home. Family members relating to one another in Christian love provide the pattern for relationships in all of the other social structures in our society.

It is essential that the Christian life express itself in the community. It is God's will that Christian concepts make an impact on the world. This will be done only as God's children bring their faith to bear on the communities in which they live. This is to be done in two ways: responsible citizenship and active witnessing.

FOR FURTHER STUDY

Farley, Gary. *The Doctrine of God.* Nashville: Convention Press, 1977, chapter 9.

Hendricks, William L. *The Doctrine of Man.* Nashville: Convention Press, 1977, chapter 8.

Stagg, Frank. *New Testament Theology.* Nashville: Broadman Press, 1962, chapters 7, 11.

Hobbs, Herschel H. *The Baptist Faith and Message.* Nashville: Convention Press, 1971.

CLYDE DENTON, JR.

When we have the hope of Christ's promise, even death is an asset rather than a liability, a blessing rather than a curse.

Chapter 8

Salvation: Ultimate Fulfillment

Christianity is a way of life. But it is a way of life that moves toward a definite goal. That goal is a joyful consummation in which the believer will experience all that he has waited for in faith. What does the life beyond this life hold in store? What is the meaning of the ultimate fulfillment that awaits the believer in the life beyond this life?

The Bible teaches that the believer's salvation will not be complete and final until the believer is in the presence of God. Paul had the ultimate and final deliverance from sin in mind when he spoke of a person's salvation being nearer than when he first believed. He encouraged the believer to look forward to and to live toward that time of final deliverance. "This do, knowing the time, that it is already the hour for you to awaken from sleep; for now salvation is nearer to us than when we believed. The night is almost gone, and the day is at hand. Let us therefore lay aside the deeds of darkness and put on the armor of light. Let us behave properly as in the day, not in carousing and drunkenness, not in sexual promiscuity and sensuality, not in strife and jealousy. But put on the Lord Jesus Christ, and make no provision for the flesh in regard to its lusts" (Rom. 13:11-14, NASB).

The future belongs to God, and he promises its fullness to those who follow him. He does not make known to us in detail what the future holds. We are expected to live toward the future in faith. God does assure us that the eternal life of the believer is in his hands. We are not to worry about the details of the future. Instead, we are to depend on God's faithfulness to keep his promises to us.

We should live each day with confident expectations about what the future holds. But as we live each day, God expects us to strive to spread the gospel and to extend his kingdom. We are able to endure the daily struggle with sin and to give ourselves to the task of living godly lives each day because of the continuing hope and assurance we have in our hearts. The hope of a final deliverance from sin and ultimate fulfillment is a hope that cannot be dispelled by critical concerns or by the power of Satan.

In the remainder of this chapter we will see that the basis of this ultimate fulfillment is Christ's incarnation, death, resurrection, and return. We will see also that some aspects of ultimate fulfillment are glorification, judgment and reward, a new heaven and a new earth, and vindication of faith.

THE BASIS OF ULTIMATE FULFILLMENT

Christ is the basis of the believer's ultimate fulfillment. Salvation from its initiation to its consummation is the work of Christ. Chapter 3 pointed out that our salvation is the result of the fact that Jesus came into the world, suffered and died on the cross, and rose from the dead. What Christ did made possible for us a new relationship with God. Christ brought about a reconciliation experience that restores persons to fellowship with the Father, a fellowship that had been lost because of sin. On the cross, Christ bore sin's penalty. This act was acceptable to God, and it was sufficient for our salvation. The seal and guarantee of this was the resurrection. The believer depends on the resurrection for the fullness of the new life. In his incarnation, Christ identified himself with man. In the crucifixion, Christ bore the sins of those with whom he had identified himself. In the resurrection, he became victor over sin and death.

After the resurrection, Christ ascended to sit at the right hand of the Father. He is now waiting for the time when he will return to bring to pass the ultimate fulfillment of believers and their final deliverance from sin. "He is the radiance of His glory and the exact representation of His nature, and upholds all things by the word of His power. When He had made purification of sins, He sat down at the right hand of the Majesty on high" (Heb. 1:3, NASB). "But He, having offered one sacrifice for sins for all time, sat down at the right hand of God, waiting from that time onward until His enemies be made a footstool for His feet. For by one offering He has perfected for all time those who are sanctified. And the Holy Spirit also bears witness to us; for after saying, 'This is the covenant that I will make with them after those days, says the Lord: I will put My laws upon their heart, and upon their mind I will write them,' He then says, 'And their sins and their lawless deeds I will remember no more' " (Heb. 10:12-17, NASB). The ultimate purpose for humanity in salvation will be realized when the exalted One returns at the end of the age.

His ascension to the Father did not mean that he left this world forever forsaken. He entered human history to make it possible for persons to be a part of the Father's kingdom. He will also return to share with his own in the consummation of history. " 'Let not your heart be troubled; believe in God, believe also in Me. In My Father's house are many dwelling places; if it were not so, I would have told you; for I go to prepare a place for you. And if I go and prepare a place for you, I will come again, and receive you to Myself; that where I am, there you may be also' " (John 14:1-3, NASB). These significant promises indelibly etch in the mind of the believer the completeness of the future life. Everyone who knows Jesus Christ as Savior will share the glory of his coming to fulfill ultimately the purpose of his Father.

Christ's promise and the Christian experience make it clear that the believer is not left an orphan by an absent Lord. The indwelling Holy Spirit gives assurance of the present, saving relationship. The Holy Spirit works in the hearts of believers to be with them, to share with them, to guide them in service, and to fulfill the promises of hope, strength, and joy.

We can live in the confidence that the ultimate fulfillment of our salvation is a certainty. Christ did all that was necessary to insure that ultimate fulfillment; he has promised us that it will happen; the Holy Spirit gives us assurance that Christ will keep his promise; and at the time of God's choosing, Christ will return to bring about the ultimate defeat of sin and the ultimate fulfillment of our salvation.

By his own divine power he keeps the believer for the salvation made ready to be revealed at the last day—that salvation that will be brought finally into ultimate consummation. Through Christ, God began our salvation; and through Christ, he will finalize it. "I am confident of this very thing, that He who began a good work in you will perfect it until the day of Christ Jesus" (Phil. 1:6, NASB). This is the hope of the believer: "In hope we have been saved, but hope that is seen is not hope; for why does one also hope for what he sees?" (Rom. 8:24, NASB). All that God has done in redemption for the believer is only the beginning of what he will do yet. What God did through Christ in redemption is the basis of our hope for what he will do ultimately.

RESULTS OF THE ULTIMATE FULFILLMENT

In the life that is beyond this life, the believer will be rescued not only from the influence of sin, but even from the presence of sin. What a liberation that will be! We shall become participants in God's eternal purposes that reach beyond creation into the glory of a restored, redeemed humanity. We shall forsake the earthly, human existence to become a part of the larger life that is one of fellowship with God the Father. This is the hope Paul spoke of with longing and with anticipation when he said, "I am hard-pressed from both directions, having the desire to depart and be with Christ, for that is very much better" (Phil. 1:23, NASB).

What does it mean to say that sin will be defeated ultimately and that the believer will be fulfilled ultimately? What effects will this produce? It is not the purpose of this chapter to delineate the sequence of events surrounding the second coming. Nor is the purpose of this chapter even to list and to explain these events. Bear in mind that this book is a study of the doctrine of salvation—not of last things. It is the purpose of the remainder of this chapter to explain what effects will be produced by Christ's final, ultimate defeat of sin and by his ultimate fulfillment of the believer. There are at least four: the believer will be glorified; the believer will be judged and rewarded; there will be a new heaven and a new earth; and faith will be vindicated.

The Believer Will Be Glorified

Glorification is one of the blessings awaiting the believer in the afterlife. And Scripture indicates that man is destined for glory. Peter wrote: "After you have suffered for a little, the God of all grace, who called you to His eternal glory in Christ, will Himself perfect, confirm, strengthen and establish you" (1 Pet. 5:10,

NASB). And Paul wrote: "For whom He foreknew, He also predestined to become conformed to the image of His Son, that He might be the first-born among many brethren" (Rom. 8:29, NASB). How tragic it is that many will not trust Christ and many others will never have the opportunity to do so, thereby missing the glory for which they were destined.

To say that the believer will be glorified in the afterlife is to say several things. Glorification means that the believer will be with Christ and will be like him. The believer will participate in the final triumph and will be a part of the endless ages. "When Christ, who is our life, is revealed, then you also will be revealed with Him in glory" (Col. 3:4, NASB).

Glorified believers will live in new and glorified bodies. They will be perfect in character and nature, freed at last from the weaknesses of the flesh. "Who will transform the body of our humble state into conformity with the body of His glory, by the exertion of the power that He has even to subject all things to Himself" (Phil. 3:21, NASB). "But now Christ has been raised from the dead, the first fruits of those who are asleep. For since by a man came death, by a man also came the resurrection of the dead. For as in Adam all die, so also in Christ all shall be made alive. So also is the resurrection of the dead. It is sown a perishable body, it is raised an imperishable body; it is sown in dishonor, it is raised in glory; it is sown in weakness, it is raised in power; it is sown a natural body, it is raised a spiritual body" (1 Cor. 15:20-22, 42-44, NASB).

The Believer Will Be Judged and Rewarded

In the history of humankind, there have been many gods and many religions. One factor common to all religions is man's belief that he is responsible to his god and that he is judged by his god. The fact of God's judgment in his dealings with humanity is evident throughout the Bible. As the one who created, preserves, and redeems, Christ has the right to be the judge of all mankind. " 'When the Son of Man comes in His glory, and all the angels with Him, then He will sit on His glorious throne' " (Matt. 25:31, NASB). " 'He has fixed a day in which He will judge the world in righteousness through a Man whom He has appointed, having furnished proof to all men by raising Him from the dead' " (Acts

17:31, NASB). "On the day when, according to my gospel, God will judge the secrets of men through Christ Jesus" (Rom. 2:16, NASB).

Judgment is a certainty for all persons—including believers. The writer of Hebrews said, "It is appointed for men to die once, and after this comes judgment" (Heb. 9:27, NASB). Lost persons and believers alike will be judged in the next life. However, there is a great contrast in the reasons for their judgments.

PERSONAL LEARNING ACTIVITY 26

Before reading further, study the following Scriptures. Decide for yourself the different reasons for which the saved and the lost will be judged. Then write a short paragraph explaining what you feel to be the difference.

Matthew 11:20-24; 25:31-46
Luke 12:42-48
1 Corinthians 3:8-15
2 Corinthians 5:6-10
Revelation 20:11-15

The reason for the judgment of the lost and the reason for the judgment of the saved are a contrast of extremes. The lost will be judged on the basis of their response to Christ. The reason for the judgment is to pronounce eternal punishment upon them because they never trusted Christ for salvation. The saved will be judged on the basis of their works. The purpose of that judgment is to determine their reward.

Earning rewards is not the primary goal of the Christian life. However, the Bible does teach that the Christian should anticipate joyfully what the future life holds in store. The saved will be rewarded. Paul wrote: "I am already being poured out as a drink offering, and the time of my departure has come. In the future there is laid up for me the crown of righteousness, which the Lord, the righteous Judge, will award to me on that day; and not only to me, but also to all who have loved His appearing" (2 Tim. 4:6,8, NASB).

PERSONAL LEARNING ACTIVITY 27

Number the actions in the following list to show what you consider to be their importance in determining a Christian's eternal reward.

____I was a Southern Baptist
____I lived a good life
____I was a faithful witness
____I attended church regularly
____I was a forgiving person
____I was a loving, Christlike parent
____I loved and respected persons of all races
____I was a kind person
____I was a hard worker
____I ministered to the poor and suffering

There Will Be a New Heaven and a New Earth
The Bible states that a new heaven and a new earth are included in God's plan of redemption. "According to His promise we are looking for new heavens and a new earth, in which righteousness dwells" (2 Pet. 3:13, NASB); "I consider that the sufferings of this present time are not worthy to be compared with the glory that is to be revealed to us. For the anxious longing of the creation waits eagerly for the revealing of the sons of God. For the creation was subjected to futility, not of its own will, but because of Him who subjected it, in hope that the creation itself also will be set free from its slavery to corruption into the freedom of the glory of the children of God. For we know that the whole creation groans and suffers the pains of childbirth together until now" (Rom. 8:18-22, NASB). "I saw a new heaven and a new earth; for the first heaven and the first earth passed away, and there is no longer any sea" (Rev. 21:1, NASB).

In spite of the language of the New Testament, it is difficult to know if God will remake this world or bring another one into existence. To argue over this point is to lose sight of the most important truths about the new heaven and the new earth. The reason for the creation of the new heaven and the new earth is far more important than how the creation will take place.

God will bring the new heaven and earth into being to provide a place of habitation for a redeemed humanity. These are the ones who have been rescued from the bondage of sin and delivered from the influence and even the presence of sin. Their habitation must be one that is equally free from the influence and the presence of sin.

We know that in this heavenly habitation we will be free from the ravaging results of sin upon our lives and upon the world in which we live. There will be no more sorrow, sickness, or death. There will be no more natural disaster. Innocent persons will no longer be caused to suffer because of evil in the lives of others. " 'He shall wipe away every tear from their eyes; and there shall no longer be any death; there shall no longer be any mourning, or crying, or pain; the first things have passed away' " (Rev. 21:4, NASB).

Being with the Father forever is another blessing the redeemed will experience in the new habitation. "We know that if the earthly tent which is our house is torn down, we have a building from God, a house not made with hands, eternal in the heavens" (2 Cor. 5:1, NASB). "I am hard-pressed from both directions, having the desire to depart and be with Christ, for that is very much better" (Phil. 1:23, NASB).

Within the heart of every Christian is a longing for unhindered, face-to-face fellowship with Christ. It is better to depart in death and be with the Lord to enjoy that thrilling experience. The believer should anticipate joyfully the blessedness of living in fellowship with the Father in a perfect environment. Not since the Garden of Eden has man had such an experience. That paradise which was lost will be regained in the eternal dwelling place of all believers.

Faith Will Be Vindicated

The Christian life is a life of faith. We committed ourselves to God through Christ because we believed. Logical facts and systematic proofs do not lie at the heart of the Christian experience. Faith to believe that God's Word is true and faith to act upon the leadership of the Holy Spirit is the foundation for conversion and Christian living. However, at the time when our salvation is complete, we will know that we were right to believe. Our faith will be vindicated.

Life is greater than death.—As a Christian, the believer commits himself in faith to the belief that God gives spiritual life and delivers from spiritual death. In the life beyond this life we shall know by personal, firsthand experience the truth of Paul's statement: "The wages of sin is death, but the free gift of God is eternal life in Christ Jesus our Lord" (Rom. 6:23, NASB).

Love is greater than hate.—The believer is committed in faith to a life of love. We believe that 1 Corinthians 13 is true. Jesus lived a life of love; he told us we should love; he made love the central principle of personal relationships; and we believe the truth of what he lived and what he taught. Jesus told us he would die for us because he loved us. He told us that that love is the motive for all that God has done for man. We have trusted Jesus, and we serve the Father because we believe in and respond to that love.

We believe that hate, the opposite of love, is always in conflict with love in the world. Hate seeks to destroy love. Because of hate, Cain killed his brother Abel. Hate displaces love in the hearts of people, destroys relationships, and destroys one's personhood. Hate sets children against parents, brother against brother, friend against friend, and nation against nation. Hate is the provocating power that leads humanity into odious and detestable acts.

Christ taught that the only force greater than hate is love. Because we believe what Christ taught, we have committed ourselves to a life of love. We believe that love will conquer hate ultimately. In the day of ultimate fulfillment, our faith in the power of love will be vindicated. We shall know that it was right to love, because we shall be participants in the eternal life where love has triumphed ultimately over hate.

CONCLUSION

Through the ages God has claimed ultimate victory. The believer has been rescued from the condemnation of sin but not from being vexed by temptations. The believer is safe from the awful consequences of sin at the day of judgment. The believer is saved from the guilt and the power of sin in this life but not from the necessity of watching and praying against it.

In this life sin limits us. Ultimately, we shall be freed from the limitations imposed by sin. In this life we possess a fallen nature and live in fallen bodies that are subject to the power of sin and Satan's attacks. In this life our bodies experience weakness, sickness, pain, and the limitation of age, and finally death itself. Ultimately, we shall possess glorified bodies that are subject to none of these limitations.

The claims of Christ, the resurrection, and our own experience give us absolute hope. When we have this hope, even death is an asset rather than a liability, a blessing rather than a curse. We can look forward with eager expectation to time's finality when our salvation will be fulfilled ultimately. When we have this hope, we can look beyond this life and cry out with Paul: "Thanks be to God, who gives us the victory through our Lord Jesus Christ" (1 Cor. 15:57, NASB). The Christian's hope of the future life is hope for ultimate victory.

PERSONAL LEARNING ACTIVITY 28
Study Luke 19:11-27. Then formulate your own answer to this question: How should the assurance of ultimate victory and fulfillment affect our lives today?

In the parable you just studied, the servants were instructed to "do business" until their master returned. We should get busy, give ourselves to ministering, and declare to the world that salvation is real. We should not sit and long for the fullness of the future. Rather, we should be involved in the life that is now.

"Do business until I return." Indeed, get busy; be my witnesses. You shall receive power when the Holy Spirit is come upon you. You will be my witnesses. You will share this message; and as you go, you will make disciples, baptizing them, teaching them the things I have taught you.

"Do business until I return." Be the salt, the light, the leaven that you should be in the world. Combat evil by being a force for right and good in the world. Be busy at the task of caring about and redeeming the whole person.

Let the redeemed of the Lord give themselves to the task of doing his business until he returns.

FOR FURTHER STUDY

Farley, Gary. *The Doctrine of God.* Nashville: Convention Press, 1977, chapter 8.

Hendricks, William L. *The Doctrine of Man.* Nashville: Convention Press, 1977, chapter 9.

Grayum, H. Frank (ed.). *Bible Truths for Today.* Nashville: Convention Press, 1970, chapter 12.

Small Group Study Guides

Bill Latham

These study guides are designed for five study sessions of one hour to one hour and fifteen minutes each. If you have less than one full hour of study time in your group, you should consider using two group meetings for each session. Otherwise, you will find it necessary to abbreviate the activities to such an extent that much of the study's effectiveness is lost. *The Doctrine of Salvation* is the text for the study. It will be used in each period. Every person should have his own copy to serve as reference and resource. To prepare to lead the study, you should do several things.

- Study the complete text carefully. Complete all personal learning activities as you study.
- Study the chapters in the books referred to under "For Further Study" at the end of each chapter in the text.
- Well in advance of the study, you should gather and/or prepare the materials you will need to lead the study. These are listed in the preparation section of the training guide for each session. In addition to those materials, you should get copies of Form 151 (Church Study Course Credit Request, Revised 1975) to request study course credit for persons in the study. Directions for requesting credit are at the end of the book.
- Make arrangements well ahead of time for the equipment you will need for your room. If at all possible, arrange to have a large room with tables and movable chairs. Try to arrange to have a freestanding chalkboard. If no chalkboard is available, arrange to have a room with ample wall space for newsprint. Arrange your room so that group members are seated comfortably and informally. Avoid having group members seated in rows. After the first session you should know approximately how many persons will be in the study. Remove all extra chairs except two or three from the room. Position tables in a semicircle or in some other arrangement so that group members can see you and one another.

UNIT WORK SHEET

A
My definition of salvation is:

B
The most important thing for me to remember about man's need for salvation is:

How would I communicate this idea to a lost person?

C
What is God's purpose for mankind and how is Christ the central figure in that purpose?

How would I communicate this idea to a lost person?

D
How would I explain to a lost person my salvation experience and the role played by the Holy Spirit in that experience?

E
How do the many different words that describe different aspects of salvation all speak of one singular experience?

F
In what setting am I strongest in living out my faith? How can I best use that strength?

How can I improve my ability to live out my faith in the setting where I have the most difficulty?

G
How will my salvation be fulfilled ultimately?

SALVATION

MAN
PARAMOUNT NE

GOD
ETERNAL PURPO

THE SAVIOR
INCARNATE MISSIO

THE HOLY SPIRIT
ENABLING ACTIO

GOD'S ACTION/MAN'S RESPON

THE TRANSFORMING EVEN

A NEW WAY OF LI

ULTIMATE FULFILLMEN

SESSION 1

Introduction and Chapter 1

Training goal: At the end of this session, each person should be able to explain in his own words why persons sin and why being rescued from the consequences of sin is a person's greatest need.

Before the Study

• Prepare the theme poster as illustrated or use the one in *The Doctrine of Salvation Resource Kit* (item 3) by glueing it to a piece of poster board.

• Get and preview the filmstrip *What Baptists Believe About Salvation.* Set up a filmstrip projector for showing the filmstrip.

• Enlist a member in advance to summarize briefly the ideas in "Where It Is All Leading" in chapter 1. Item 4 in *The Doctrine of Salvation Resource Kit* provides a slip for making this assignment.

• Prepare copies of the unit work sheet as illustrated or use the ones provided in *The Doctrine of Salvation Resource Kit* (item 5). Prepare enough copies for each member to have a work sheet.

• Have on hand extra copies of *The Doctrine of Salvation.*

• Have on hand pencils and note paper.

• Have on hand enough front-page sections from your local newspaper for each person to have a section.

• Prepare a series of posters as follows. At the top of a piece of poster board, write one of the meanings of sin given in the chart in chapter 1 of the text. Prepare a separate piece of poster board for each meaning of sin given in the chart. *The Doctrine of Salvation Resource Kit* contains strips for preparing these posters (item 6). Before the first session in the study, attach these posters to the walls at different places in the room.

• If this is a new group, have on hand registration materials and name tags.

During the Study

• If this is a new group, ask members as they arrive to register and to prepare name tags.

• As members arrive, distribute copies of *The Doctrine of Salvation* to those who do not already have copies.

• If this is a new group, spend a few minutes getting to know the members and helping them get to know one another.

• Explain the course requirements for receiving study course credit for this study. (See the explanation at the end of the book.)

• Use the theme poster to preview the entire study. State the title and training goal for each session and give a brief explanation of the central idea in each chapter. The introduction to the book contains one set of summary statements. Then explain the procedure you will follow to lead each session of study.

• Distribute copies of the unit work sheet. Ask members to keep this work sheet with their Bibles and textbooks throughout the study. Ask, What is salvation? Allow time for only a few responses. Then ask each person to write in section A of the unit work sheet his own definition of salvation. When members have had time to finish writing, ask them to compare and discuss their definitions. Then ask members to turn to the definition at the beginning of the textbook and compare it to the definitions they have been discussing.

• Ask each person to review personal learning activity 3 in the textbook. Ask any who have not already completed the activity in their preparation to complete as much as possible while the other members review.

• Call attention to the posters you have fastened to the walls of the room. Give each person a copy of the front-page section of your local newspaper with instructions to tear out articles that describe or relate to the different kinds of sin described in personal learning activity 3. After about five minutes, make several rolls of transparent tape available and ask members to stick the articles to the appropriate posters.

• Briefly survey the articles that have been fastened to the posters. Then call attention to the fact that the author of the text describes persons' sins as corruptive wrongdoing. Ask members to discuss whether they agree that sins can be characterized accurately by this phrase. Then ask: Do you think the clippings support this characterization of sins? Why?

• Introduce and show frames 1-18 of the filmstrip *What Baptists Believe About Salvation.* Ask: If you were Pastor Talbot, how would you answer Bob's question? Why does sin separate from God? Ask members to discuss in groups of three what their answer would be. After a brief work time, ask the groups to suggest answers to Bob's question. Then show frames 18-24 of the filmstrip and ask members to compare their answers to ideas in the filmstrip. (If the filmstrip is not available, ask members to discuss in groups of three why sin separates from God. Refer to "What Man Is Doing to Himself" in chapter 1 as a resource for this discussion. After time for discussion, ask the groups to compare and discuss their answers.

• Read Luke 6:43-45 aloud. Ask, What did Jesus say about the real reason persons sin? Allow time for a brief discussion. Be sure the discussion includes the major ideas discussed in "Why He Does It" in chapter 1. Point out any ideas not brought out in the discussion.

• Observe that the last part of chapter 1 deals with the consequences of sin and the fact that those consequences begin in this life. Call on the member enlisted in advance to summarize briefly the ideas in "Where It Is All Leading" in chapter 1.

• Ask each person to complete section B on his unit work sheet. Use the remaining time for members to share what they have written on their work sheets.

• Urge each person to study carefully chapters 2 and 3 in *The Doctrine of Salvation* before the next session and to complete all personal learning activities in those chapters.

• Close with prayer that the study will be meaningful for each person.

SESSION 2
Chapters 2 and 3

Training goal: At the end of this session, each person should be able to explain in his own words God's purpose for mankind and how Christ is the central figure in that purpose.

Poster 1	Poster 2	Poster 3
Psalm 8:1-3 Colossians 1:16-17	Isaiah 46:6 Galatians 3:6-9	2 Corinthians 4:4 Titus 3:5

Before the Study

• Display the theme poster.

• Prepare three small posters as illustrated. *The Doctrine of Salvation Resource Kit* provides copies of these posters (item 7).

• Have newsprint, tape, and crayon or a chalkboard available.

• Enlist one person to explain what God's purpose means to man. An assignment slip for this assignment is available in *The Doctrine of Salvation Resource Kit* (item 4).

• Enlist three persons to serve on a panel to discuss redemption's revelation. Ask these to study carefully "Redemption's Revelation" in chapter 3. Give each a copy of the questions you will ask. Ask each to be prepared to discuss each question and to make frequent use of the Scriptures as he does. Assignment slips for this assignment are available in *The Doctrine of Salvation Resource Kit* (item 4).

• Prepare listening assignment slips to give group members immediately before the panel discussion. The assignment should be to listen and to list reasons that Christ is the central figure in God's purpose for man. These slips are available in *The Doctrine of Salvation Resource Kit* (item 4).

During the Study

• Welcome and register any new members.

• Use the theme poster and the training goal to introduce this session.

• Say, God's purpose is to bring us home again to himself. Then show small poster 1. Ask members to locate and read these passages in their Bibles. Then ask, In what way do these verses show that God has revealed his purpose? (*creation*) Then lead member to discuss briefly how creation reveals God's purpose of redemption.

• Follow the same procedure with small posters 2 and 3. The response to poster 2 should be *history of Israel;* and the response to poster 3 should be *incarnation.*

• Call on the person enlisted in advance to explain what God's purpose means to man. Ask each member to listen as the explanation is given and to be prepared to suggest what he feels is the most significant statement made.

• After the explanation, ask, What do you feel was the most significant statement in the explanation of what God's purpose means to man? List members' responses on a piece of newsprint fastened to the wall or on the chalkboard. (Do not expect members to agree on a single statement. A number of statements probably will be suggested.) Call attention to the fact that a number of suggestions have been made. Ask members to discuss why they are all significant.

• State that the last part of chapter 2 deals with how God fulfills his purpose. Give a brief summary of this section. Then explain that the remainder of the book deals with how God fulfills his eternal purpose for man.

• Ask members to recall the title of chapter 3. Then ask, Why did Jesus come to earth to make salvation possible? List members' responses on the chalkboard or on another piece of newsprint. Then ask members to discuss their responses. (Responses should include the main ideas in "Redemption's Why and How" in chapter 3. Call attention to any ideas that members do not recall.)

• Distribute listening assignment slips to members. Seat panel members at the front of the room and use the following questions to moderate a discussion of redemption's revelation.

1. Read John 1:1. Ask: When God brought salvation to humanity through Christ, it was his thought and feeling toward man being crystallized. How is this true? What were his thought and feeling?
2. The text says that in Christ God really gave us the facts about himself. How is this true?
3. By his incarnation, what did Christ reveal about himself?
4. How was Christ the supreme revelation of grace?
5. The text also states that Christ revealed the ultimate truth. What was that truth?

• Read Romans 4:25 and briefly summarize the main points in "Redemption and Resurrection" in chapter 3.

• Ask members to complete section C on their unit work sheets. After members complete the assignment, ask volunteers to share what they have written.

• Close with sentence prayers, asking for a deeper appreciation for God's love and grace and a more complete understanding of the meaning of the incarnation.

SESSION 3
Chapters 4 and 5

Training goal: At the end of this session, each person should have written how he would explain to a lost person his own salvation experience and the part played by the Holy Spirit in that experience.

Before the Study

• Display the theme poster.

• Enlist members to present the information in "The Holy Spirit Brings the Sinner to Salvation" and "The Holy Spirit Continues the Work of Salvation in the Believer" in chapter 4. Ask each person to prepare a poster as illustrated for use with his presentation.

The Holy Spirit Brings the Sinner to Salvation	**The Holy Spirit Continues the Work of Salvation in the Believer**
Enables the sinner to see his need	Presence
Convicts of sin	Power
Convicts of righteousness	Assurance
Convicts of judgment	Hope of adoption
Enables the sinner to see the Savior	Seal of promise
Brings the sinner out of death to life	Earnest

These posters and assignment slips for the assignment are available in *The Doctrine of Salvation Resource Kit* (items 8 and 4).

• Write on a sheet of newsprint fastened to the wall or on the chalkboard: If left alone, man not only would remain separated from God; he would not even be aware of the separation.

• Have paper and pencils available.

• Set up a filmstrip projector to show *What Baptists Believe About Salvation.*

During the Study

• Begin with prayer for an increased awareness of and responsiveness to the presence of the Holy Spirit in the lives of members.

• Ask all members to stand and move quickly and quietly outside the meeting room. When all members are gathered outside the room a short distance from the entrance, give these instructions: We are all to go back into the room and find our seats without speaking or helping any other person. And we are to do so with our eyes closed. Try to find your seat without opening your eyes until your are seated. If you must give up and open your eyes, you still should not speak to or assist any other person. (If the group is too large for every person to engage in this activity, use several volunteers while the remainder of the group members observe without speaking or helping.)

• When all members are seated and have opened their eyes, call attention to the statement you have written on the newsprint or on the chalkboard. Explain that the purpose of the opening activity was to help members gain insight into the difficulty a person has trying to find his way to God without the spiritual insights and assistance given by the Holy Spirit. Ask members to imagine how much more difficult the assignment would have been if someone had rearranged the room while they were outside or if they had been taken to a place they had never been before and were told to find their way out without the benefit of sight.

• Use the theme poster, the training goal for this session, and the introduction to chapter 4 to begin this study session.

• Call on the persons enlisted in advance to explain how the Holy Spirit brings sinners to salvation and how the Holy Spirit continues the work of salvation. After each explanation ask members to discuss what has been said.

• Explain that you are going to lead the group to discuss what must happen to enable salvation to take place. Ask members to use the information in the filmstrip they will see and in chapter 5 of the text as resources for their discussion. Ask members to recall the portion of the filmstrip they have seen. Show frames 25-50 of *What Baptists Believe About Salvation.*

• Distribute paper and pencils to group members. Ask each person to draw a line down the center of his sheet and to list on one side all the things God has done and continues to do to bring salvation to pass. After members have worked a few minutes, ask them to compare and discuss the things they have listed. Ask members to recall Scriptures that substantiate the things they have listed.

• Say, There is no doubt that salvation is God's work. Your lists show that he initiates and carries out the experience. In fact, it almost would appear that the individual has nothing to do with it. But he does. List on the other side of your sheet all the things a person must do to bring salvation to pass. After members have completed their lists, lead them to compare and to discuss what they have written. The discussion should include the main ideas in chapter 5. Call attention to any points the members overlook. Ask members to recall Scriptures to substantiate the things they have listed.

• Ask members to recall the three witnesses to salvation discussed in chapter 5. List these on the chalkboard. Then ask volunteers to share with the group how they have experienced these witnesses in their lives.

• Instruct members to complete section D on their unit work sheets. After a brief work period, ask volunteers to share what they have written.

• Urge members to study chapter 6 carefully before the next study session. State that a supply of concordances, study Bibles, Bible dictionaries, and Bible commentaries will be needed for the next session. Ask members to volunteer to bring as many of these resources as possible.

• Close with prayer that each person will have an opportunity to share his testimony with some lost person.

SESSION 4
Chapter 6

Training goal: At the end of this session, each person should be able to explain how the many terms used to describe the different aspects of salvation all speak of one singular experience.

Before the Study

• Display the theme poster.

• Write the following headings at the tops of seven sheets of newsprint—one heading per sheet.

Regeneration
Conversion
Forgiveness and Justification

Reconciliation
Adoption
Sanctification
Perseverance

Strips for preparing these sheets are available in *The Doctrine of Salvation Resource Kit* (item 9).

• Have crayons and tape available.

• Get a supply of concordances, study Bibles, Bible dictionaries, and Bible commentaries. Ask your pastor to help you locate these resources. You may need to borrow from other church libraries or from other pastors in your community.

• Prepare seven assignment slips as illustrated.

> Use chapter 6 in *The Doctrine of Salvation* and the other resources to prepare a definition of the term on your sheet of newsprint and to discover what aspect of salvation that term describes. Write your definition on the newsprint and be prepared to explain to the group what aspect of salvation the term describes. You will have only five minutes to report. So, be brief and to the point.

Assignment slips for the assignments are provided in *The Doctrine of Salvation Resource Kit* (item 4).

During the Study

• Begin with prayer for a deeper understanding of all that is involved in salvation.

• Use the theme poster, the training goal, and the introduction to chapter 6 to begin this study session.

• Form seven work groups (even if the size of your group requires that some of these be one-person work groups). Distribute to the groups the sheets of newsprint you have prepared, crayons, study resources, and assignment slips.

• After about fifteen minutes, reassemble the group and call for reports. As each group reports, attach its sheet of newsprint to the wall. After each report, allow members to ask questions.

• Ask each person to complete section E on his unit work sheet.

After members have completed the assignment, allow volunteers to share what they have written.

• Close with sentence prayers, thanking God for the difference salvation makes.

• Urge members to study carefully chapters 7 and 8 before the next session.

SESSION 5
Chapters 7 and 8

Training goal: By the end of this session, each person should have identified ways he can improve his ability to live out his Christian faith in different settings. He should be able to explain how his salvation will be fulfilled ultimately.

Before the Study

• Display the theme poster.

• Enlist members to prepare and to act out the following situations.

Role play 1: Two persons are talking. One is a faithful church member. The other feels that church membership is not important to being a good Christian. The faithful church member gives testimony to what being a part of the church has meant to him. The other person argues against taking church seriously.

Role play 2: An adult and a child are talking about the importance of being Christian in the home. They discuss what having a Christian home has meant to them, and they recall some of the difficulties they have faced.

Role play 3: Two Christians are talking. One believes that religion should be kept inside the church and not mixed with business or with politics. The other is explaining why he feels it is important to express his faith in the context of daily life.

Make the persons enlisted aware of the ideas they are expected to communicate in their role play; ask them to use the appropriate sections in chapter 7 as a resource to prepare. Role-play scripts are available in *The Doctrine of Salvation Resource Kit* (item 10). These scripts can be learned, they can be used as a guide in preparing more original scripts, or they simply can be read.

During the Study

• Use the theme poster and the training goal to begin this session.

• Call for the three role-play situations. After each, use these questions to stimulate discussion around the ideas in that role play. Why is it important to live out your Christian faith in this setting? What factors make it difficult to do so? How can you overcome the difficulties you face in living out your Christian faith in this setting?

• Instruct each person to complete section F on his unit work sheet. After members have completed the assignment, ask volunteers to share what they have written.

• Use the introduction to chapter 8 to move into the final part of the study.

• Then ask, What is the basis of our salvation's ultimate fulfillment? Allow time for responses and discussion.

• Ask members to read 1 Corinthians 15:20-22,42-44 and discuss what those verses say about our ultimate salvation. (*Believers will be glorified.*)

• Lead members to work together to complete personal learning activity 26 in chapter 8.

• Read Revelation 21:1 and ask, Why will God bring the new heaven and the new earth into being?

• Briefly summarize "Faith Will Be Vindicated" and ask members to share with the group the greatest joy they have found as a result of salvation.

• Instruct members to complete section G on their unit work sheets.

• Lead members in singing "I Know that My Redeemer Liveth" and lead in prayer, asking God to help group members lead others to find the joy of salvation in Christ.

The Church Study Course

The Church Study Course consists of a variety of short-term credit courses for adults and youth and noncredit foundational units for children and preschoolers. The materials are for use in addition to the study and training curriculums made available to the churches on an ongoing basis.

Study courses and foundational units are organized into a system that is promoted by the Sunday School Board, 127 Ninth Avenue, North, Nashville, Tennessee 37234; by the Woman's Missionary Union, 600 North Twentieth Street, Birmingham, Alabama 35203; by the Brotherhood Commission, 1548 Poplar Avenue, Memphis, Tennessee 38104; and by the state conventions affiliated with the Southern Baptist Convention.

Study course materials are flexible enough to be adapted to the needs of any Baptist church. The resources are published in several different formats—textbooks of various sizes, workbooks, and kits. Each item contains a brief explanation of the Church Study Course and information on requesting credit. Additional information and interpretation are available from the participating agencies.

Types of Study and Credit

Adults and youth can earn study course credit through individual or group study. Teachers of courses or of foundational units also are eligible to receive credit. Reading the book is required for study course credit.

1. *Class experience.*—Group involvement with course material for the designated number of hours for the particular course. A person who is absent from one or more sessions must complete the Personal Learning Activities for each session missed.
2. *Individual study.*—This includes reading, viewing, or listening to course material and completing the specified requirements for the course.
3. *Lesson course study.*—Parallel use of designated study course material during the study of selected units in Church Program Organization periodical curriculum units. Guidance for this means of credit appears in the selected periodical.
4. *Institutional study.*—Parallel use of designated study course material during regular courses at educational institutions, including Seminary Extension Department courses. Guidance for this means of credit is provided by the teacher.

Credit is awarded for the successful completion of a course of study. This credit is granted by the Church Study Course Awards Office, 127

Ninth Avenue, North, Nashville, Tennessee 37234, for the participating agencies. Form 151 (available free) is recommended for use in requesting credit.

When credit is issued to a person on request, the Awards Office sends to the church two copies of a notice of credit earned. The original copy of the credit slip should be filed by the Study Course Records Librarian in the participant's record of training folder. The duplicate should be given to the person who earned the credit. Accumulated credits are applied toward leadership or member development diplomas, which are measures of learning, growth, development, and training.

Detailed information about the Church Study Course system of credits, diplomas, and record keeping is available from the participating agencies. Study course materials, supplementary teaching or learning aids, and forms for record keeping may be ordered from Baptist Book Stores.

The Church Study Course Curriculum

Credit is granted on those courses listed in the current copy of Church Services and Materials Catalog, the Church Study Course Catalog, and Baptist Book Store Catalog. When selecting courses or foundational units, the current catalogs should be checked to determine what study course materials are valid.

How to Request Credit for This Course

This book is the text for a course in the subject area Baptist Doctrine.

The course is designed for five hours of group study. Credit is awarded for satisfactory class experience with the study material for the minimum number of hours. A person who is absent for one or more sessions must complete the Personal Learning Activities for each session missed.

Credit also is allowed for use of this material in individual study and in lesson course study and institutional study if so designated.

After the course is completed, the teacher, the Study Course Records Librarian, or any person designated by the church should complete Form 151 (Church Study Course Credit Request, Revised 1975) and send it to the Awards Office, 127 Ninth Avenue, North, Nashville, Tennessee 37234. Individuals also may request credit by writing the Awards Office or by using the special coupon on the last page of this book.

Reading the book is required for study course credit.

INSTRUCTIONS: If requested by the teacher, fill in this form and give it to him when the course is completed. If preferred, mail this request for course credit to

AWARDS OFFICE
THE SUNDAY SCHOOL BOARD, SBC
127 NINTH AVENUE, NORTH
NASHVILLE, TENNESSEE 37234

State Convention	Association	Indicate Type of Study (X)
		☐ Class ☐ Individual ☐ Lesson Course ☐ Educational Institution

CHURCH	MAIL TO
Church Name	Mail to (If Different from Church Address)
Mailing Address	Street, Route, or P.O. Box
City, State, Zip Code	City, State, Zip Code

LAST NAME	FIRST NAME AND MIDDLE INITIAL	MRS. (X)	COURSE TITLE
			The Doctrine of Salvation

Cut along this line